HOW
to
BEGIN
the
CHRISTIAN
life

GEORGE SWEETING

MOODY PUBLISHERS
CHICAGO

Interior design: Ragont Design
Cover design: Kathryn Joachim
Civer image: iStock © hypergon 2007

ISBN: 978-0-8024-3582-8

We hope you enjoy this book from Moody Publishers. Our goal is to provide high-quality, thought-provoking books and products that connect truth to your real needs and challenges. For more information on other books and products written and produced from a biblical perspective, go to www.moodypublishers.com or write to:

Moody Publishers
820 N. La Salle Boulevard
Chicago, IL 60610

1 3 5 7 9 10 8 6 4 2

Printed in the United States of America

CONTENTS

"For which one of you, when
he wants to build a tower,
does not first sit down and calculate
the cost to see if he has
enough to complete it?"

Luke 14:28 nasb

HOW TO USE THIS BOOK

- *Read it alone.* Do not try to digest all of the material in one evening. Read a chapter a day if possible. The important thing is to understand it and apply it. Relate it to your job, your school, your family, and your church.
- *Another possibility is to study it with someone else.* Secure another copy for a friend who has begun the Christian life. Spend a few hours of the day or an evening each week together.
- *Use it in a group study.* For example,

  in your church's new members class
  as an elective in Sunday school
  in a home Bible study
  as a Sunday evening training program for home
      visitation
  as a high school elective study course
  in follow-up classes for your camping programs
      for junior and senior high teens
  in adult vacation Bible school classes

These studies have been used by pastors and laypeople literally around the world in new-convert and church-membership classes. They have also been used in teenagers' meetings, in early morning men's and women's Bible study classes, and even for family devotions.

There are many other ways to use this book, but, whatever way you choose, remember to

read it carefully,
read it prayerfully,
read it systematically,
and read it completely.

May God bless you as you grow in the Christian life.

Watch your beginnings! The right start in the Christian life can greatly encourage your rate of growth and increase your future usefulness and enjoyment. It is of supreme importance to start right.

"Being confident of this, that he who
began a good work in you
will carry it on to completion until
the day of Christ Jesus."

PHILIPPIANS 1:6 NIV

Foreword

YOUR FIRST STEPS

YOU, MY FRIEND, have taken a life-changing step. You have decided to begin a new life. God has become your heavenly Father, and you are now His child; a wonderful eternal relationship has begun. It is really a brand-new beginning. In the words of Jesus, you have been "born again."

Possibly you feel helpless to explain what has taken place. A new sense of freedom is yours. You are something like a happy child let loose in a big park. Practically everything is touched with divine newness, and it is delicious. You now have a new hope, a new outlook, and a new attitude toward everything.

Do not be perplexed by what you have experienced, for this is wonderfully normal and right. The apostle Paul puts it this way: ". . . if anyone is in Christ, he is a new creation; the old has gone, the new has come!" (2 Corinthians 5:17 NIV). When you receive Jesus Christ, you become a brand-new person. You came alive spiritually!

Lyle Dorsett shares D. L. Moody's own words about his first steps.

> I remember the morning on which I came out of my room after I had trusted Christ. I thought the old sun shone a good deal brighter than it ever had before—I thought that it was just smiling upon me: and as I walked out upon Boston Common and heard the birds singing in the trees, I thought they were all singing a song to me. Do you know, I fell in love with all creation. I had not a bitter feeling against any man, and I was ready to take all men to my heart.[1]

WHAT YOU HAVE DONE

1. *You have acknowledged your need as a sinner.* What is this decision that you have made? You have acknowledged that you were wrong and that God is right. You have agreed with God that you yourself are spiritually bankrupt. You have told the Lord of the poverty of your soul. Earnestly you have prayed, "God, be merciful to me, a sinner!" (Luke 18:13 ESV). Your first step was to acknowledge your need as a sinner.

Dead and *lost* are the two Bible words used to describe your past life. Dead things can't grow. You do not grow *into* grace; you grow once you are in it. Nothing is so completely helpless as that which is dead, and as far as God is concerned, all people through natural birth are spiritually dead. The Bible describes your spiritual transformation this way: "And you He made alive, who were dead in trespasses and sins" (Ephesians 2:1). Your life has been changed from a dead to a living state in Christ. God has touched your life and imparted divine life—His life—eternal life. This decision is really a life-changing decision.

Lost is a descriptive word. The Bible states, "For the Son of Man has come to seek and to save that which was lost" (Luke 19:10). Without Christ we are lost like sheep without a shepherd—helpless, hopeless, and defenseless; we are lost like the prodigal son—separated, destitute, and disgraced. By your decision you have been changed from a lost to a found condition, changed from an enemy of God to a friend of God, changed from a stranger to a child of God. Your salvation is revolutionary.

Seneca, the Roman philosopher, said, "We have all sinned, some more, some less." Coleridge, the great thinker, confessed, "I am a fallen creature." T. S. Eliot's character Cecilia Copplestone talks about her "awareness of solitude" and "a sense of sin." John Stott, prior to his conversion, wrote to a friend and confessed, "I know the kind of person that I want to be. But I feel defeated. I fall short of my own ideals."[2] The Bible plainly says, "All have sinned and fall short of the glory of God" (Romans 3:23 NIV).

2. *You have acknowledged Jesus Christ as your Savior.* The Lord Jesus Christ came into this world to meet our basic need. Christ was born to die. "This is a faithful saying, and worthy of all acceptance, that Christ Jesus came into the world to save sinners" (1 Timothy 1:15 KJV). This purpose was accomplished when He died on the cross. Repeatedly, Jesus told His disciples of His intended death. On the night of His betrayal by Judas, He broke bread with His disciples. Plainly, He explained to them the purpose of the cross. "For this is My blood of the new covenant, which is shed for many for the remission of sins" (Matthew 26:28). Paul simply and clearly wrote, "For He made Him who knew no sin to be sin for us, that we might become the righteousness of God in Him" (2 Corinthians 5:21). Isaiah prophetically penned, "But He was wounded for our transgressions, He was bruised for our iniquities; the chastisement for our peace was upon Him, and by His stripes we are healed" (Isaiah 53:5).

Our basic need is the forgiveness of sin. God's provision for our need is found in the death of Jesus Christ. Jesus Christ, the sinless Son, fully and completely bore the sins of the world. He took upon Himself our sin. The gospel is the good news of what God has done through Christ to forgive our sins.

Recognizing Christ as God's answer, that He died in your place, you have come asking forgiveness for all your sins. "For Christ also suffered once for sins, the just for the unjust, that He might bring us to God" (1 Peter 3:18). In a definite act of faith, you have pledged your allegiance to Christ. At that moment, Jesus became your Savior, and God forgave your sins.

The word *confess* is interesting. It simply means "to speak the same thing." It means "to agree or acknowledge." You have first acknowledged your need as a sinner, but you have secondly acknowledged Jesus Christ as your personal Savior and Lord. What have you done? You "have believed" (John 20:29).

3. *You are now beginning to acknowledge Jesus Christ before others.* You may ask, "Do I have to publicly confess Christ?" I must answer, "Yes, Jesus Christ requests a public confession." And I might ask, "How can we help it?"

Jesus plainly said, "Whoever confesses Me before men, him I will also confess before My Father who is in heaven" (Matthew 10:32). If you have sincerely trusted Christ, you will want to tell others about it. This new life will be obvious, for "out of the abundance of the heart the mouth speaks" (Matthew 12:34).

Some new Christians try to be "secret" believers, but this is unwise and wrong. Imagine Dr. Jonas Salk keeping his polio vaccine a secret! This would have been criminal. So, too, a knowledge of God's salvation places us in debt to the whole world.

Both Nicodemus and Joseph of Arimathea tried to be secret disciples. It took Jesus' death to bring them to the place of openly begging His body from Pilate. The Scripture record is clear: "After this, Joseph of Arimathea, being a disciple of Jesus, but *secretly*, for fear of the Jews, asked Pilate that he might take away the body of Jesus; and Pilate gave him permission. So he came and took the body of Jesus. And Nicodemus, who at first came to Jesus by night, also came, bringing a mixture of myrrh and aloes, about a hundred pounds. Then they took the body of Jesus, and bound it in strips of linen with the spices, as the custom of the Jews is to bury" (John 19:38–40).

Do not let your fear of others rob you of the joy of

open allegiance. It is sin to be silent when to confess would help another.

To be ashamed of Christ is a sad experience. It implies carelessness and failure on our part. It dishonors Christ and brings personal defeat. If Jesus Christ were ashamed of you and me, which we could easily understand; but for men and women to be ashamed of Christ is difficult to comprehend. Joseph Grigg asks,

> Jesus, and shall it ever be,
> A Mortal man ashamed of Thee?
> Ashamed of Thee, whom angels praise,
> Whose glories shine through endless days?
>
> Ashamed of Jesus! Sooner far
> Let evening blush to own a star;
> He sheds the beams of light divine
> O'er this benighted soul of mine.
> Ashamed of Jesus! That dear friend
> On whom my hopes of heaven depend!
> No; when I blush, be this my shame,
> That I no more revere His name.
>
> Ashamed of Jesus! yes, I may,
> When I've no guilt to wash away;

No tear to wipe, no good to crave,
No fears to quell, no soul to save.

Ashamed of Christ? We must never be. Repeatedly we are encouraged in Scripture to confess Christ openly and not be ashamed. Jesus said, "For whoever is ashamed of Me and My words in this adulterous and sinful generation, of him the Son of Man also will be ashamed when He comes in the glory of His Father with the holy angels" (Mark 8:38). To be reproached for Christ now is to be rewarded later. At times we may be called upon to share in Christ's sufferings. This really implies that He and we are together. "If anyone suffers as a Christian, let him not be ashamed" (1 Peter 4:16), writes Peter.

I have found that failure to acknowledge Jesus often results in careless living, whereas a public commitment puts one on record before God and man. The fact that others know of your decision will help guard you against temptation.

Yes, your decision is a life-changing one. With Philip Doddridge you can say,

O happy day that fixed my choice
On Thee, my Saviour and my God!

Well may this glowing heart rejoice,
And tell its raptures all abroad.
Happy day, happy day,
When Jesus washed my sins away!

Yes, your decision has begun a happy, lasting change. You are ready to build a new life for the glory of God.

WHAT YOU MUST DO NOW

As a newborn baby is cared for in the physical world, you need to be helped spiritually. Let me list some helpful steps that I will enlarge upon in later chapters.

1. *Read the Bible systematically.* What food is to the body, the Bible is to your new spiritual life. At a regular time, in a quiet place, each day should start with the Bible. This is a *must* if you are to grow in the things of God. The gospel of John is a good place for you to begin. Remember, at least a chapter a day! D. L. Moody said, "The Bible will keep you from sin or sin will keep you from the Bible." A chapter a day will certainly help to keep sin away.

2. *Learn to pray.* Prayer is the communion of the believer with God; we speak to God, but He also

speaks to us. Prayer is not merely asking favors of God but, rather, waiting in quietness before Him. Pray for personal cleansing and victory over evil; pray for yourself and pray for others.

3. *Use every opportunity to confess Christ before the world.* In a winsome way, immediately tell someone of your spiritual decision. Activity strengthens. When believers share with others, they develop an appetite for Bible study. The result of their speaking to others of their new life will provide daily, up-to-date subjects for prayer. When a new Christian begins working, everything comes into proper focus. R. A. Torrey said, "The more you make of Jesus Christ, the more he will make of you. It will save you from many temptations if the fact is clearly known that you are one who acknowledges Christ as Lord of all things."[3]

4. *Become part of a local church.* If a mother permits her children to grow up in idleness, the result will be unprepared children. Since the Christian's responsibilities toward other believers is clear, waiting only forms bad habits. The Bible says, "Not forsaking the assembling of ourselves together, as is the manner of some" (Hebrews 10:25). Your faithful church attendance will help you in spiritual growth. Find a church that gives full allegiance to Jesus Christ

and the Word of God, and *become part of it.*

If you follow these four Bible steps, Christian growth is promised. You will be sure to meet temptations, but you need not yield or fall to them, for God has promised, "He who is in you is greater than he who is in the world" (1 John 4:4). If you do fall, ask for immediate forgiveness. "If we confess our sins, He is faithful and just to forgive us our sins and to cleanse us from all unrighteousness" (1 John 1:9). If you fall, don't remain defeated but get up and go on. Perhaps right now you are facing a battle with some attitude or habit; remember that Jesus is ready to help you, and He has *all power* in heaven and earth.

Another important lesson for successful Christian living is to keep your eyes on Jesus. The best of Christians will fail you, but never forget—"Jesus never will!" CONGRATULATIONS on your decision to receive Jesus Christ as your Savior. Now strive to follow these first steps. *Starting right* is a key to spiritual growth.

QUESTIONS

1. What is the first step in receiving Jesus Christ as Savior?
2. Give two Bible words that describe our past sinful condition.

3. What is the second step in receiving Jesus Christ as Savior?
4. What does the word *confess* mean?
5. Give at least two verses of Scripture that indicate we should publicly confess Jesus Christ before others.
6. List four steps that will aid spiritual growth.

NOTES

1. Lyle W Dorsett, *A Passion for Souls* (Chicago: Moody, 1997), 49–50.
2. Roger Steer, *Basic Christian* (Downers Grove, Ill.: InterVarsity Press, 2009), 34.
3. R. A. Torrey, *How to Succeed in the Christian Life* (New York: Revell, 1906; Chicago: Moody, n.d.)

REMINDERS

Watch your beginnings! It is of supreme importance to start right.

Dead things cannot grow. You do not grow into grace; you grow once you are in it.

The gospel is the good news of what God has done through Christ to forgive our sins.
A knowledge of God's salvation places us in debt to the whole world.

"The Bible will keep you from sin or sin will keep you from the Bible," said D. L. Moody.

R. A. Torrey said, "The more you make of Jesus Christ, the more he will make of you."

"Being confident of this, that he who began a good work in you *will carry it on to completion* until the day of Jesus Christ." —Philippians 1:6 NIV

"But as many as received Him, to them He gave the right to become children of God, to those who believe in His name: **who were born**, not of blood, nor of the will of the flesh, nor of the will of man, but **of God**."

John 1:12–13

A Christian is the combination of Christ and you. If we take the first three words of John 1:13 and the last two words,we have the phrase "who were born . . . of God." A Christian is **one . . . who is born of God**.

1

WHAT IS A CHRISTIAN?

IN SCORN AND RIDICULE the world gave birth to the word *Christian*. In Antioch of Syria, a city of half a million inhabitants, the followers of Jesus were given this nickname. The word *Christian* appears only three times in the New Testament and never in the Old Testament. First occurring in Acts 11:26, "And the disciples were first called Christians in Antioch," it appears again in Acts 26:28, "Then Agrippa said to Paul, 'You almost persuade me to become a Christian,'" and again in 1 Peter 4:16, "Yet if anyone suffers as a Christian, let him not be ashamed, but let him glorify God in this matter."

To be a Christian in the early centuries was a life-and-death challenge; it was a faith for heroes. To be a Christian meant at times facing a pagan arena and wild beasts; it also meant a narrow gate, a straight way, the denial of self, shouldering a cross and following Jesus.

WHAT IS A CHRISTIAN?

1. *To be united with Christ.* The word *Christian* is really the combination of two words: *Christ* and *man*. When a man or woman is united with Christ, he or she forms one word—*Christian.* A Christian is the combination of *Christ* and *you.* The sinner receives the Savior, and the Savior receives the sinner. A Christian is a "Christ man" or a "Christ woman."

2. *To be born again.* When Jesus spoke to Nicodemus He said, "Unless one is born again, he cannot see the kingdom of God" (John 3:3). According to Jesus, a Christian is one who has been *born again.* Spiritual birth is the only way to enter God's family; *we must* be born again.

In our day, the word *Christian* has been seriously corrupted. It has been pulled and stretched to cover the whole civilized world. Often it has been misused, misapplied, misunderstood, and misappropriated. Thousands call themselves Christians who have no claim to the name at all. Some say, "All civilized people are Christians." Others suppose this word includes all Gentiles and excludes all Hebrews. To the contrary, there are many splendid people who are Jewish and

Christian, and, sad to say, there are thousands of Gentiles who are not Christians at all. The concept of Christianity has become so distorted that millions do not know the difference between true spiritual salvation and mere religious profession.

The story is told of some American seamen marooned on a South Sea island. Fearing the natives, the sailors hid, until one day they heard some of the inhabitants speaking perfect English. In relief, the marooned men falsely exclaimed, "They are Christians!"

In reality, no one has the right in his unforgiven state to say, "I am a Christian."

You ask, "But why?" Because the Bible teaches that "all have sinned."

God's justice and holiness demand that sin be paid for and dealt with. Jesus, God's Son, voluntarily died to atone for the sins of all mankind. When one receives Jesus in faith, then, and only then, does that one have the right or the scriptural authority to be a child of God. John the apostle said, "But as many as received Him, to them He gave *the right* to become children of God, even to those who believe in His name" (John 1:12).

3. *To receive Christ as Savior.* To receive Christ is to have faith in Him, that He is the sinless Son of God, that He died voluntarily for our sins so that we might be free from spiritual death and judgment and have everlasting life. The all-important question is, Have you made this decision? Have you received Jesus Christ as your Savior?

A WORD OF WARNING

Religion is popular in our day. The world is full of people who say, "I believe in God. I believe in Jesus, and I believe in the Bible." Sometimes the lives of these do not correspond with what they claim to believe. For the most part, this is not a saving faith but a false faith.

The Bible says, "Faith without works is dead" (James 2:20), and again, "By their fruits you will know them" (Matthew 7:20). So, if there is no difference, no distinction, I fear that some individuals are in the flesh, and will "reap corruption" (Galatians 6:8).

In all probability, there's not a prisoner in the world who does not believe it is better to be honest. There is not a drunkard who does not believe it is better to be sober. But mere belief does nothing to change the condition. Faith has come to be thought of today as a simple acquiescence to the Word of God. But this kind of faith is paralyzing and deadening. The Bible reminds us, "Even the demons believe—and tremble!" (James 2:19). The difference between heart belief and head belief is the difference between being saved and lost. Any faith that does not result in a changed life is not a saving faith; it is a deceiving faith. So the important question to ask is, "Have I believed savingly?"

Occasionally there are those who claim they cannot believe what they do not understand. But in reality we believe much that we do not understand. For example, no one understands the mysteries of electricity, yet it would be foolish to say, "I will sit in darkness until I understand electricity."

No doctor completely understands the marvels of the digestive system. Yet, who would say, "I will not eat until I understand the digestive system"?

Who understands the miracle of the common watermelon? A seed is dropped into the ground. It sprouts, and soon there is a vigorous plant that bears several watermelons, each of which is hundreds of times the weight of the original seed. Outside of each there is a beautiful coat of green, then a rind of white and an enticing core of red with dozens of seeds, each capable of producing additional watermelons. The most brilliant person cannot explain this mystery, but the most ignorant can enjoy it.

So when you submit to the gospel, you become part of the divine mystery. You are quickened by God and become "a new creature." Jesus said, "The wind blows where it wishes, and you hear the sound of it, but cannot tell where it comes from and where it goes. So is everyone who is born of the Spirit" (John 3:8).

By way of review:

1. A Christian is one who is "united with Christ."
2. A Christian is one who has been "born again."
3. A Christian is one who has "received Jesus Christ."

WHAT A CHRISTIAN IS NOT

Sometimes we understand the positive better by considering the negative. I remember well the happiness of my own boyhood experience. On Sunday, all six of us children accompanied Mother and Father to church; our meals were always prefaced with family prayer; we read the Bible systematically. Ours was a Christian home, yet this wonderful inheritance did not automatically make me a Christian. Relationship to the redeemed does not bring redemption. Kinship to Christians cannot make one a Christian. God's salvation is *not* by natural birth. *God doesn't have any grandchildren.* John 1:13 shares three errors that exist today: "Who were born, not of blood, nor of the will of the flesh, nor of the will of man, but of God."

1. *Natural birth cannot make one a Christian:* "who were born not of blood."

John is simply saying that one does not become a Christian through our earthly parents. The blessing of a godly mother and father is a great heritage, but this does not make one a Christian. Parents can give a good push in the right direction, but they cannot make their children Christians.

The Jewish people used to say, "We have Abraham as our father," and therefore they thought they were safe and secure. The exponents of Nazism boasted of pure "Aryan blood" and talked of a "superrace." This, too, is unscriptural. In the Bible the mystery of blood is in the heritage of sin, derived from Adam by natural birth. It is also in the gift of salvation purchased by the blood of Christ through spiritual birth. John the apostle is saying that no one can become a Christian through earthly parents. Natural birth cannot make one a Christian.

2. *Good works cannot make one a Christian:* "nor of the will of the flesh."

Probably the greatest error that exists today is the belief that salvation is the result of *personal effort.* Thousands imagine themselves Christian because they seek to keep the Golden Rule or because they live decent, moral lives. Some rely upon their religious activity or church membership. In direct contrast, the apostle John says that salvation does not come through "the will of the flesh."

I once asked a faithful church attender if she were a Christian. She quickly answered, "I have taught in the Sunday school for sixteen years."

I commended her and kindly repeated the question. "Are you a Christian?"

She then told me of her efforts in the missionary program but did not answer my simple question. This individual was depending on *her own efforts* to earn salvation. If being active in religious work makes one a Christian, she would be one many times over; but the Bible says, "not of the will of the flesh."

The Bible message is plain and easy to understand.

Paul said, "By grace you have been saved through faith, and that not of yourselves; it is the gift of God, not of works, lest anyone should boast" (Ephesians 2:8–9). Salvation is not *something* you do but *Someone* you receive. Salvation is a relationship with Jesus Christ.

It would be easier to tunnel through the mountains with teaspoons than to get to heaven by personal effort, character, or morality. Salvation is *an offer, not a demand*. It is not based on what *I do* but on what Jesus Christ *has done*.

We do not become Christians by climbing the ladder of good works, rung by rung. In fact, the very opposite is true. Jesus came down the ladder via Bethlehem's manger and Calvary's cross to meet us where we are. Good works cannot make one a Christian.

3. *Religious ordinances cannot make one a Christian:* "nor of the will of man."

Some time ago I asked a medical doctor, "Are you a Christian?" He answered, "I was baptized by Dr. So-and-so years ago." After further discussion, I learned that he was banking everything on the ordinance of baptism rather than upon his personal faith in Christ. No man, no matter how prominent or pious, can make you a Christian. The false idea that some religious leader can make one a Christian by some religious act is contrary to the teaching of the Bible. No church sacrament of ordinance, however important, can forgive sin.

Evangelist D. L. Moody once said, "I freely admit salvation is worth working for. It is worth a man's going round the world on his hands and knees, climbing its mountains, crossing its valleys, swimming its rivers, going through all manner of hardship in order to attain it, but we do not get it that way. It is to him that believes."[1]

Ministers are instruments of God to perform His will. As Paul said, "we are God's fellow workers" (1 Corinthians 3:9). "We are ambassadors for Christ, as though God were pleading through us: we implore you on Christ's behalf, be reconciled to God" (2 Corinthians 5:20). Never can any man confer salvation or forgiveness upon another.

Being a Christian is much more than believing certain doctrines or submitting to any ordinance. *It is receiving Christ.*

WHAT A CHRISTIAN OUGHT TO BE

For the apostle Paul, salvation and surrender were simultaneous. Immediately upon believing, he asked, "Lord, what do You want me to do?" (Acts 9:6). Just as

Paul wanted to do God's will only, so every Christian should commit his entire life to Christ. Paul called upon all Christians to "present yourselves to God" (Romans 6:13). Adolph Deissman suggested that the word *Christian* means "slave of Christ," as *Caesarian* meant "slave of Caesar."

In the Old Testament, God promised Abraham that he would be the father of a great nation, with children as numerous as the sand of the sea. But Abraham had no children. Contrary to the life of faith, he fathered a son by Hagar, his wife's slave. This act was of the flesh, representing man's blundering way rather than God's way. God intervened and performed a miracle. In her old age, Abraham's wife Sarah gave birth to Isaac, a child of faith, the fulfillment of God's eternal plan.

God calls each Christian to let go of his own solutions to life's problems and accept the way of faith. He is really saying, "Don't hang on to anything; *yield everything.*"

It is a big mistake to imagine that you can carelessly ramble along in the Christian life. As Samuel Rutherford said, "You will not be carried to Heaven lying at ease upon a feather bed." Tertullian said, "He who fears to suffer cannot be His who suffered."

The call of Christ while on earth was uncompromising and unconventional. His words were so piercing that the hearers tried to kill Him. Yet today, we often present the Lord of glory as meek and mild rather than high and holy, as soft and sentimental instead of steadfast and strong. Artists and poets have occasionally portrayed Jesus with flowing chestnut hair, breathing mild benedictions upon everyone. This is false! It is true that He went about doing good; but on the other hand, He was firm and His words were stringent. At times He gave offense to His disciples, to His relatives, to the scribes and Pharisees. On one occasion, Jesus said, "Do not think that I came to bring peace on earth. I did not come to bring peace but a sword" (Matthew 10:34).

True, He was loving and kind, but we must not overlook the demands of His call. "Now it happened as they journeyed on the road, that someone said to Him, 'Lord, I will follow You wherever You go.'"

Jesus answered the enthusiastic offer with a staggering response: "Foxes have holes and birds of the air have nests, but the Son of Man has nowhere to lay His head."

Another cried, "Lord, let me first go and bury my father."

The reply struck back as fast and devastating as lightning. "Let the dead bury their own dead, but you go and preach the kingdom of God."

A third cried, "Lord, I will follow You, but let me first go and bid them farewell who are at my house."

Jesus dealt a crushing blow when He said, "No one, having put his hand to the plow, and looking back, is fit for the kingdom of God" (Luke 9:57–62).

The Christian life is a great adventure, but it is not a picnic. Jesus never gained disciples under false pretense. He never hid His scars but rather declared, "Behold My hands and My feet" (Luke 24:39).

John Koessler says it well, "Paul compared the life of discipleship to the rigors of military training or athletic competition. The opportunity to endure is also the opportunity to experience God's grace. God uses hardships and endurance to transform us into the image of Christ."[2]

From history's pages we learn of a cowardly young soldier in the army of Alexander the Great. Whenever the battle grew fierce, the young soldier would retreat. The general's pride was cut because this timid soldier also bore the name Alexander. One day Alexander the Great pointedly rebuked him, saying, "Stop being a coward, or drop that good name."

The call to each Christian is the same today. May we live up to all that the name *Christian* implies.

QUESTIONS

1. How many times does the word *Christian* appear in the Bible and where?
2. Give two definitions in answer to the question, "What is a Christian?"
3. List three errors that exist in our world today, according to John 1:13.
4. According to John 1:12, what happens to the person who receives Jesus Christ?
5. According to Acts 9:6, a Christian ought to be what?
6. What did Paul call all Christians to do, in Romans 6:13?

NOTES

1. Sam Paxton, *Short Quotations of D. L. Moody* (Chicago: Moody, 1961).
2. John Koessler, *True Discipleship* (Chicago: Moody, 2003).

REMINDERS

A Christian is the combination of *Christ* and *you.*

The difference between heart belief and head belief is the difference between being saved and lost. God doesn't have any grandchildren.

Salvation is an offer, not a demand.

Jesus never gained disciples under false pretense. He never hid His scars but rather declared, "Behold My hands and My feet."

"But grow in the grace and knowledge of our Lord and Savior Jesus Christ."

2 Peter 3:18 niv

"How does the soul grow? Not all in a minute! Now it may lose ground, and now it may win it; Now it rejoiceth, and now it bewaileth; Now its hopes fructify, then they are blighted; Now it walks sullenly, now gropes benighted; Fed by discouragements, taught by disaster; So it goes forward, now slower, now faster, Till all the pain is past, and failure made whole, It is full grown, and the Lord rules the soul."

Susan Coolidge

"We ought always to thank God for you, brothers, and rightly so, because your faith is growing more and more, and the love every one of you has for each other is increasing."

2 Thessalonians 1:3 niv

2

HOW TO GROW IN
THE CHRISTIAN LIFE

SOME TIME AGO I READ a book titled *Grow Up or Blow Up*. The thrust of the book was that civilization must either grow up or else destroy itself. It is equally necessary that we as individuals "grow" in the things of God.

Our century finds the masses of people living and dying for material possessions. An unparalleled wealth fever infects the majority, while spiritual values are often ignored. But the true measure of success in life is not and cannot be counted in dollars and cents and surely not in physical and mental accomplishments. In complete contrast, the true and eternal measure of life is found in spiritual growth. You will find this road to be a neglected one. There are no superhighways to growth.

Robert Browning said, "Man was made to grow, not stop." Peter and Paul believed the same thing. Peter challenged all Christians to "grow in the grace and knowledge of our Lord and Savior Jesus Christ" (2 Peter 3:18). The preceding verse contains a stern warning: "Beware lest you also fall from your own steadfastness, being led away with the error of the wicked." Immediately following the warning appears God's cure for falling: "Grow in grace."

Romans 8:29 also encourages every believer "to be *conformed* to the image of His Son." Ephesians 4:15 tells us to "*grow up* in all things into Him." First Thessalonians 3:12 challenges us to "*increase* and abound."

THE FIRST STEP OF GROWTH IS LIFE

Dead things cannot grow. Before there can be spiritual growth, there must be spiritual life. When a child is born, the first cry indicates life. If there is life, a world of possibilities beckons to this new baby. If there is no life, *there is no hope*. A fence post placed in the ground will not grow, but a little seed will grow spontaneously. Drop a stone into the richest soil and it will be exactly the same size years later. Place a seed into the ground, and it will spring up and produce a stalk and flowers. The difference is plain: one has life while the other does not. LIFE is essential for growth.

The divine life may be imitated, but the difference is easily detected. One is real; the other is false. One is natural; the other is mechanical. The crystal grows from without by addition of new particles, while a living organism grows from within. The crystal may be beautiful, but it is only a crystal and lacks true life for growth. *Dead things may accumulate, but they cannot grow.*

Unless men and women have the life that comes from above, religious practices and environment mean nothing. In fact, they cause a person to rest in a false hope, making judgment more sure. To you who have received Jesus Christ, God's divine command is "Grow in grace." Those to whom Peter is speaking have been "born again," for, remember, dead things cannot grow.

The story is told of a young sixteenth-century artist who worked hard and long on a statue of an angel. The famous Michelangelo was invited to view the finished masterpiece. As Michelangelo studied it, he commented, "It lacks only one thing . . . and that is *life*, it would be as perfect as God could make it."

Yes, *God's life* is the starting place and the first step for growth.

WHY YOU MUST GROW

1. *It is God's plan.* God said to Moses, "Be holy, for I am holy" (Leviticus 11:45). Jesus also said, "You

shall be perfect, just as your Father in heaven is perfect" (Matthew 5:48). Paul, speaking to the Philippians, wrote,

> Not that I have already attained, or am already perfected; but I press on, that I may lay hold of that for which Christ Jesus has also laid hold of me. Brethren, I do not count myself to have apprehended; but one thing I do, forgetting those things which are behind and reaching forward to those things which are ahead, I press toward the goal for the prize of the upward call of God in Christ Jesus. (Philippians 3:12–14)

Rather than being complacent, Paul was reaching, stretching, and pressing forward. Growth is not just the dream of a starry-eyed idealist; it is rather *God's plan* for each believer. Growth is God's will for us.

2. It is nature's law. Nature says, "Grow, or I will kill you." A diseased tree eventually does not send forth new shoots. When the body stops growing, it begins to die. The fingers of nature begin to pick and to pluck til death claims us. The first law of life is expansion. It's grow or decay! Advance or regress! Live or die! Jesus said, "Every branch in Me that does not bear fruit He takes away; and every branch that bears fruit He prunes, that it may bear more fruit" (John 15:2).

We are instructed by Scripture to "grow in grace." The word *grow* speaks of continuous action. There is not time to stop growing. If we do not grow in the physical realm, it is a sad sign; it is a mark of sickness. A mother would be alarmed if day after day and week after week her baby showed no signs of growth. A farmer would be dismayed if his crops never yielded a harvest.

Genesis 11:31 tells us that Terah started out with Abraham for the land of Canaan. Verse 31 reads, "And they came to Haran and *dwelt there.*" Verse 32 says, "Terah died in Haran." It sometimes seems that too many today are stopping at Haran and dying there. There is no time or place to stop growing. Growth is according to God's plan and nature's law.

HOW TO GROW

1. *Naturally.* Jesus said, "Why do you worry about clothing? Consider the lilies of the field, *how they grow*: they neither toil nor spin; and yet I say to you that even Solomon in all his glory was not arrayed like one of these" (Matthew 6:28–29).

Notice the phrase "how they grow." Well, how do the lilies grow? What is their secret of growth? The lily, according to God's plan, simply unfolds the life within. We do not tell a lily to grow; it grows *naturally*, spontaneously. It does not fuss or fret, toil or turn, strain or stretch; it just grows. Growth is natural and inevitable *when there is life*, and more so when there is *divine life*.

Environment is an important factor in the growing process. If I see an acorn lying on the sidewalk, I know that the acorn will never grow, but put the acorn in the ground where it belongs and it will grow. If we tear a plant out of the soil and hide it from the sun, it will not grow. In just the same way, we who have received Christ must abide in Him if we are to grow and be fruitful.

The child of God must continue in a right relationship with God. We are to be *rooted* in the Word of God. We are to be *warmed* by the Son of Righteousness. We are to *make friends* of God's children. We are to cooperate in every way with the *divine Gardener*. Do not permit anyone or anything to come between you and the Lord. Keep "looking unto Jesus, the author and finisher of our faith" (Hebrews 12:2). Then we will bring forth fruit, "a hundredfold, some sixty, some thirty" (Matthew 13:8).

Salvation is just *the beginning* of what God wants to do for you. He "is able to do exceedingly abundantly above all that we *ask or think*, according to the power that works in us" (Ephesians 3:20). Before each believer is the limitless ocean of grace and truth. May we never be content with the empty shells on the beach, when we can launch out in the deep.

The Bible compares Christians to trees. Our roots penetrate the topsoil of truth and stretch down into the great doctrinal rocks of eternal salvation. Then when the hurricane of God's judgment blows upon the unbelieving, only those trees planted by God will stand.

As trees we need to throw back our heads and look to Jesus for refreshment. We need to spread our branches and let the shadow of our holy influence be felt far and near. Our branches should be heavy with fruit. God's promise is,

I will be like the dew to Israel; *he shall grow like the lily*, and lengthen his roots like Lebanon. His branches shall spread; his beauty shall be like an olive tree, and his fragrance like Lebanon. Those who dwell under his shadow shall return; they

shall be revived like grain, *and grow like a vine.*
Their scent shall be like the wine of Lebanon.
(Hosea 14:5–7)

2. *We grow by eating.* All living things eat, and
what we eat affects our growth. The Bible says, "Eat
what is good" (Isaiah 55:2). No book will make you
grow like the Bible.

If we placed the most costly silk under a micro-
scope, it would appear rough and stained. However,
the petal of a lily, under the same lens, is flawless.
Solomon's royal robes could not compare with God's
wild lilies. The lily's threadlike roots dig down to the
minerals and practice *selection.* Some minerals look
fine, but in reality they are hurtful. They must be
refused. Others are necessary and they are received.
This is exactly what we must do to grow in grace.

There are appealing things that are deadly to
growth. The apostle Peter points out some things to
refuse: "Laying aside all malice, all deceit, hypocrisy,
envy, and all evil speaking." Others are to be received:
"As newborn babes, desire the pure milk of the word,
that you may grow thereby" (1 Peter 2:1–2). Whatever else it means, it means that the Word of God is
good to feed on. Milk is a food that has been digested

by another. Often Christians think that the only feeding they need is that which the pastor or others have digested and presented. That is good, but not enough. "You search the Scriptures, for in them you think you have eternal life; and these are they which testify of Me" (John 5:39).

We are to feed on the meat of the Bible. D. L. Moody used to hoe potatoes as a boy. He said that he hoed them so poorly he always had to place a marker where he stopped hoeing. I wonder if we occasionally read the Bible that way?

3. We grow by breathing. What breathing is to the physical person, prayer is to the spiritual person. Jesus was a man of prayer. The common atmosphere was stifling to Him, and so He frequently sought communion with God in places apart from the crowd. If Jesus, the sinless Son of God, found prayer important, we sinful creatures dare not live without it.

I agree with R. C. Sproul's comment: "Prayer is to the Christian what breath is to life, yet no duty of the Christian is so neglected."[1] Archbishop Trench reminds us, "Prayer is not overcoming God's reluctance: it is laying hold of His highest willingness."[2] Yes, we will grow if there is regular communion with Jesus. He is our life!

Rubinstein, the great pianist, said, "If I omit practice one day, I notice it; if two days, my friends notice it; if three days, the public notices it." This truth is still relevant. We are instructed to "pray without ceasing" (1 Thessalonians 5:17). Someone else has said, "Prayer is *the preface* to the book of Christian living, *the text* of the new life sermon, *the girding on of the armor* for battle, *the pilgrim's preparation* for his journey; and it must be supplemented by *action* or it amounts to nothing."

Prayer and work form the unbeatable New Testament combination. True prayers, seldom come creeping home empty-handed. We agree with Fanny Crosby's gospel song:

> Oh, the pure delight of a single hour
> That before Thy throne I spend,
> When I kneel in prayer, and with Thee, my God,
> I commune as friend with friend!

4. We grow by resting. This is what Jesus was talking about when He asked, "Which of you by worrying can add one cubit to his stature?" (Matthew 6:27). Anxiety will not add to your spiritual development; worry will not add one fraction to your maturity.

The Christian life is not a nervous, hanging-onto-God but rather a resting-in-the-hollow-of-His-hand. We will not grow by toiling and turning, stretching and straining but rather by yielding to Christ's control.

If we have God's life and avail ourselves of the Bible and prayer, growth will be natural and inevitable. The Bible urges us to "Rest in the Lord, and wait patiently for Him" (Psalm 37:7). "Underneath are the everlasting arms" (Deuteronomy 33:27). "He gives His beloved sleep" (Psalm 127:2). "The righteous shall flourish like a palm tree, he shall grow like a cedar in Lebanon. Those who are planted in the house of the Lord *shall flourish* in the courts of our God. They shall *still bear fruit in old age*; they shall be fresh and flourishing" (Psalm 92:12–14).

5. *We grow by exercising.* The Bible places considerable emphasis on *work*. Show me a person who will not work, and I will show you a person who is *underdeveloped.* On the other hand, if you faithfully work, you will eat and sleep right. People occasionally complain that they are not spiritually fed, but possibly they are not spiritually hungry, and they are often not hungry because they are not working. Broken-down tissues call for nourishment. If a believer will sincerely serve in God's world, he will grow strong.

Friend, if you really long to grow, begin *to work*. Practice the truth you know, and many other things will become clearer. The farmer's arms become strong by continual labor. The child grows by exercise. We are to grow as babies grow: slowly, steadily, and surely; a little each day, and a lot in a year. At first the legs will be weak, but soon we will walk without being weary and run without fainting. "Whoever has, *to him more will be given*" (Mark 4:25). Jesus said, "My Father has been *working* until now, and I have been *working*" (John 5:17).

One good way to exercise is to witness concerning our faith in Jesus Christ. Jesus plainly said, "You shall be witnesses to Me" (Acts 1:8). A witness is one who tells what he knows. After everything is said and done, our REAL excuse for living is to be a witness. Witnessing keeps our prayer life alive and up-to-date. It also challenges us to dig into the Scripture in search of answers for those to whom we are witnessing.

My friend, since your conversion, have you been growing? Are you glorifying God more now than last week? Are you more committed now than at your conversion? Is your delight in the law of the Lord and are you meditating upon it day and night?

With God's help, Christians can be like trees

planted by the rivers of water, spreading forth foliage and bearing fruit. Apart from Christ, we are chaff, without hope and substance.

I encourage you to grow, grow, grow until that exciting future day when we shall see Him and be like Him!

> If God can make of an ugly seed,
> With a bit of earth and air
> And dew and rain, sunshine and shade,
> A flower so wondrous and fair,
> What can He make of a soul *like you*,
> With the Bible and faith and prayer,
> And the Holy Spirit, if you do His will
> And trust in His love and care.
> —Author Unknown

John Koessler reminds us, "God is the ultimate source of all spiritual development, but He has chosen to use specific means to promote it. Chief among them are prayer and the Scriptures. Those who neglect the appointed means of growth and fail to practice Christian virtues will see their spiritual lives decline. Grace previously acquired may disappear. They may even begin to question whether there was ever a genuine transformation in their lives in the first place. When they ought to be mature enough to teach others, they will need to go back to kindergarten and learn the first principles of the Christian life all over again."[3]

QUESTIONS

1. What is the very first necessary step for growth?
2. Give three verses that show that God intends Christians to grow.
3. Why is a study of the Bible compared to food?
4. Illustrate from the life of Jesus the importance of prayer.
5. What effect can witnessing have on prayer and Bible study?
6. List five suggestions for growth.

NOTES

1. R. C. Sproul, *Following Christ* (Wheaton: Tyndale House, 1984), 108.
2. Quoted in Frank S. Mead, comp., *The Encyclopedia of Religious Quotations* (New York: Books, Inc., 1965).
3. John Koessler, *True Discipleship* (Chicago: Moody, 2003), 121

REMINDERS

Dead things cannot grow. Before there can be spiritual growth, there must be spiritual life.

We need to grow because growth is God's plan. We must bend or be broken.

Salvation is just the beginning of what God wants to do for you.

No book will make you grow like the Bible.

According to Archbishop Trench, "Prayer is not overcoming God's reluctance: it is laying hold of His highest willingness."

Prayer and work form the unbeatable New Testament combination. True prayers never come creeping home empty-handed.

Thank God for the spiritual growth you have experienced. Ask the Lord for help to grow increasingly like Jesus.

"Do you not know that you
are the temple of God and that
the Spirit of God dwells in you?"

1 Corinthians 3:16

When Dwight L. Moody was visiting En-
gland, he heard Henry Varley say, "The world
has yet to see what God can do with and for
and through a man who is fully and wholly
consecrated to Him . . ." A man!
"Varley meant any man. Varley didn't say he
had to be educated, or brilliant, or anything
else. Just a man. Well, by the Holy Spirit in
me I'll be that man."

J. C. Pollock, *Moody*

J. C. Pollock, *Moody: A Biographical Portrait* (Grand
Rapids: Zondervan, 1963), 99.

3

YOU AND
THE HOLY SPIRIT

EVERY CHRISTIAN MUST rely on the Holy Spirit because He is indispensable to living the Christian life. He is the chief architect in building a successful life. And yet, for many people, the Holy Spirit is the forgotten member of the Trinity. His ministry is either unknown or ignored, and His power is unused.

A. W. Tozer wrote, "The idea of the Spirit held by the average church member is so vague, as to be nearly nonexistent."[1]

In the preface to his paraphrase of the New Testament Epistles, J. B. Phillips writes,

The great difference between present-day Christianity and that of which we read in these letters is that to us it is primarily a performance, to them it was a real experience . . . To these men it is quite plainly the invasion of their lives by a new quality of life altogether. They do not hesitate to describe this as *Christ "living in" them.*[2]

What a rebuke to us! As I read this I could not help but ask myself, "What kind of Christian am I? Am I experiencing the all-powerful presence of God the Holy Spirit?"

Down through the centuries, there have been many examples of Christians who, although their lives were quite ordinary, were transformed by the power of the Holy Spirit into vibrant and energetic witnesses for Jesus Christ.

The apostle Peter is a striking example of an average disciple transformed into a dynamic witness on the day of Pentecost. Prior to Christ's death, he denied Jesus three times, yet after Pentecost he displayed supernatural courage.

Some time ago I received a letter from a young man. "For twenty of my thirty-three years," he wrote, "I have been a professing Christian. But not until recently did I really understand the work of the Holy Spirit, what He could do in my life. The difference He has made in my life has been unbelievable."

Each believer must realize that the Holy Spirit dwells within and that He is willing and waiting to be our Helper, Teacher, and Guide. Conversion to Jesus Christ *began* in us with the generating power of the Holy Spirit, and it *continues* and will *conclude* by His life-giving resurrection power.

THE HOLY SPIRIT IN THE OLD TESTAMENT

During Old Testament times, the Spirit of God was active but apparently in a more limited way. For example, He was present in creation, for the Scripture says, "And the Spirit of God was hovering over the face of the waters" (Genesis 1:2). Of Samson we read, "And the Spirit of the Lord came mightily upon him" (Judges 14:6). Then, too, certain men were said to possess the Spirit of God. For instance, "The Lord said to Moses, 'Take Joshua the son of Nun with you, a man in whom is the Spirit, and lay your hand on him'" (Numbers 27:18).

The Old Testament contains at least eighty-eight references to the Holy Spirit. These references seem to show that the Holy Spirit would come for a specific task and then leave when the work was complete. In the New Testament the relationship to the Holy Spirit is constant and abiding.

The Spirit of God was the Spirit of conviction while sin worked itself out from fall to flood; He was a Spirit of detailed service while the people of God were being organized into a nationality; He was a Spirit of strength while the people were fighting for the land, and were casting out those who had deeply sinned; and He became a Spirit of hope when the peculiar people had passed into a condition of apostasy and wandering. He lit the horizon with the glow of approaching day.[3]

THE HOLY SPIRIT AS PROMISED BY JESUS

There is no doubt that the Spirit of God was active in the Old Testament; however, Jesus promised that the Holy Spirit would come in a greater way than ever before. In fact, Jesus said that it was expedient, or *better*, for His disciples that He go away, for if He did not go away, the Spirit would not come (John 16:7).

John the apostle verified this when he said that the Holy Ghost was not yet given "because Jesus was not yet glorified" (John 7:39). This passage appears to indicate that the Holy Spirit was to come and be active in a greater way than ever before. The fulfillment of this promise took place at Pentecost.

In the first chapter of the book of Acts, the disciples were commanded to wait for the coming of the

Holy Spirit. The second chapter tells the thrilling story of His arrival (Acts 2:1–4).

From that day to this the Holy Spirit has never departed. He has been with the church ever since. Often He is grieved because of our unbelief, but He is *never* absent. Pentecost marked the coming of the Spirit *to live* in the earthly bodies of all believers. Joyfully we can sing:

> O spread the tidings 'round, wherever man
>   is found,
> Wherever human hearts and human woes
>   abound;
> Let every Christian tongue proclaim the
>   joyful sound;
> The Comforter has come! —Frank Bottome

THE HOLY SPIRIT IS A PERSON

The Holy Spirit possesses all the characteristics of personality. He has intellect and will. He possesses emotion. He is not some vague force. He is not an impersonal power or energy like electricity or gravity.

The Holy Spirit is also our *Teacher.* "But the Helper, the Holy Spirit, whom the Father will send in My name, He will teach you all things, and bring to your remembrance all things that I said to you" (John 14:26).

The Holy Spirit assures us of personal salvation. In Romans 8:16 we read, "The Spirit Himself bears witness with our spirit that we are children of God." The Holy Spirit agrees with our spirit if we are in tune with God.

Again in John 16, Jesus taught that the Holy Spirit convinces men of sin. When the Holy Spirit comes, said Jesus, "He will convict the world of sin, and of righteousness, and of judgment" (v. 8).

The Holy Spirit teaches us, strengthens us, witnesses within us. Yes, the Holy Spirit has particular characteristics and functions. The Bible clearly teaches that *He is a person.*

THE HOLY SPIRIT INDWELLS ALL BELIEVERS

The Bible plainly teaches that each believer is the dwelling place of the Holy Spirit. What a staggering truth! Think of it—God the Holy Spirit indwelling every Christian!

To the immature Corinthians, Paul wrote, "Do you not know that you are the temple of God and that the Spirit of God dwells in you?" (1 Corinthians 3:16). In spite of their carnality, they were still the dwelling place of the Holy Spirit.

In past history God dwelt in the tabernacle and then later in the temple. You may ask, "Where does He dwell now?" The Bible says "in you"—"Christ in you, the hope of glory" (Colossians 1:27). Whether you are eight years of age or eighty, the moment you receive Christ, the Holy Spirit takes up His dwelling in your earthly body.

The word *dwell* is a beautiful term. It means to settle down and live, as you would at home. The Holy Spirit is a personal, permanent guest. He is with us and in us *all the time.*

As a living resident within the believer, the Holy Spirit gives strength for our weaknesses. He guides us in understanding God's Word and God's will. He helps us to pray. He empowers us to serve. He comforts us in our sorrow. He is the Paraclete, the one sent to assist us in every conceivable area of our lives.

More happened when you received Jesus than you ever realized. First, you received the forgiveness of sins. Second, you instantly became a member of the great family of God. Third, you were sealed with the Holy Spirit. Paul said, "In whom also, having believed, you were sealed with the Holy Spirit of promise" (Ephesians 1:13). This speaks of divine ownership.

Paul continues, "For the temple of God is holy,

which temple you are" (1 Corinthians 3:17). Paul is simply telling us that our lives must be holy. Always remember, He is the Holy Spirit, and He requires cleanness of life. The Bible says, "Walk in the Spirit, and you shall not fulfill the lust of the flesh" (Galatians 5:16).

THE HOLY SPIRIT
AND THE STRUGGLE AHEAD

There is within every Christian a *conflict.* The apostle Paul gives us a picture of this in Romans 7. Although the believer has been completely forgiven, he soon discovers that sin is still active within him. Although we are changed because of conversion, we are not all that we shall be someday. Sin continues to work in us, and the result is a battle between the "new nature" with all its new ideals and aspirations and the "old nature" with its desires and expectations. The Christian wants to please God, whereas the unconverted man seeks to please himself.

Is there a way out? Are we destined to be victims of our sinful natures, or can we be victors? What a thrill it is to know that *victory is absolutely possible*! It is available to all.

First, to be victorious you must submit your life to

Jesus Christ and receive Him as Savior. Someone has said, "If you would master temptation, you must first let Jesus master you."

Mankind is like a clock whose mainspring is broken. He needs to be totally renewed on the inside, but the repairs must be supplied from without. He cannot save himself. Even so, men and women today need someone to remake them. That someone is Jesus Christ, the Redeemer of man's soul and nature. He loves you, He died for you, and He wants you to turn to Him in repentance and faith. Salvation is the first step to victory over temptation.

Second, to the believer—the child of God—is given the privilege of prayer in overcoming temptation. James says, "if any of you lacks wisdom, let him ask of God, who gives to all liberally and without reproach, and it will be given to him" (James 1:5).

Do you need help in overcoming your weakness? Ask God! Do you need deliverance from the power and temptation of sin? Ask God! He alone is able to deliver you. Often I have cried out, "Lord, help me," and God's deliverance was given. Nothing is too great for Him.

God's Word proclaims that "no temptation has overtaken you except such as is common to man; but

God is faithful, who will not allow you to be tempted beyond what you are able, but with the temptation will also make the way of escape, that you may be able to bear it" (1 Corinthians 10:13).

D. L. Moody once said, "Whenever the great tempter of souls comes down upon us, God will give us the will, the power and the grace to overcome him and to grow stronger for the victory. Of himself, a man has not the power, but God will give him the better over all temptations if he only asks Him to do it."[4]

Third, apply the Word of God. Jesus put Satan to flight by quoting Scripture. Jesus said, "It is written," and so must we fortify ourselves with the Word of God.

Fourth, submit to the indwelling Holy Spirit. When a drop of water falls on a hot stove, the water never really touches the stove. It rests on a thin cushion of very hot air. Heat overcomes gravity and holds the water away until it evaporates. To the child of God who is directed by the Holy Spirit, temptation may come but it will not be able to destroy us. For God has promised, "He who is in you is greater than he who is in the world" (1 John 4:4).

In your hour of trial, remember that God is faithful. He knows your capacity. He will give you all the strength you need to overcome temptation, or He will make a way of deliverance for you.

Leonard Ravenhill has written, "The greatest miracle that God can do today is to take an unholy man out of an unholy world, and make that man holy, and put him back into that unholy world, and keep him holy in it!"

The secret of victory in your Christian life is the *indwelling Holy Spirit.* Allow Him to have undisputed control of your whole life.

THE HOLY SPIRIT EMPOWERS FOR SERVICE

A. C. Dixon used to say, "When we rely on organization, we get what organization can do. When we rely upon education, we get what education can do. When we rely on eloquence, we get what eloquence can do. But when we rely on the Holy Spirit, we get *what God can do.*"

Power is within the reach of all who believe. Our departing Lord said, "But you shall receive power when the Holy Spirit has come upon you" (Acts 1:8).

I heard a true story not long ago of a man who for several years had struggled to keep his rather large lawn mowed. Finally he decided it just wasn't worth all the time and trouble. He determined that he was going to buy one of those nice riding lawn mowers, something that would take all the headache out of his Saturday afternoons.

The day came for the delivery of his new machine. The man who brought it told him just how it should be operated, explaining all the controls, and also pointed out that it was already filled with gas and oil.

Well, the man could hardly wait to try out his new mower. As soon as the delivery man left, he jumped into the seat and turned the key, but nothing happened. No engine started, no noise, nothing!

His first reaction was to check the gas and oil. They were fine. Then he examined the key and turned it back and forth. Still nothing! Finally he decided that despite the fact that the mower was brand-new, the battery must be dead. So he took the battery to the nearest service station and had it charged, came home, turned the key—and again nothing happened.

As he was just about to reach his wits' end, his neighbor came over and asked him what his trouble was. After explaining all he had been through, the neighbor climbed onto the mower, turned the key, pushed the starter, and immediately the engine began to purr. The owner was completely flabbergasted! To think he had all that trouble simply because he failed to *push the starter button*!

"How simple!" you say, and you are absolutely right! But what the starter button was to that lawn mower, the Holy Spirit is in the life of the believer. Just as the machine needed the contact of power to operate, so we need the power of the Holy Spirit to live and serve successfully in the Christian life.

As you depend on the Holy Spirit, you shall be empowered to live above the world, the flesh, and the devil. In your own strength you will surely fall, but "if by the Spirit you put to death the deeds of the body, you will live" (Romans 8:13). The Holy Spirit is your source of power.

A WORD OF WARNING

We must always remember that the Holy Spirit may be grieved because of careless living. Paul warns, "Do not grieve the Holy Spirit of God, by whom you were sealed for the day of redemption" (Ephesians 4:30). The word *grieve* means to "cause sorrow." G. Campbell Morgan asks, "How would you like to be compelled to live with somebody who was everlastingly grieving your heart by his conduct?" Do not grieve or quench the indwelling Holy Spirit; rather, "Be filled with the Spirit" (Ephesians 5:18). Allow God the Holy Spirit complete control of your life.

The Holy Spirit is our Helper today, tomorrow, and always. Open wide every area of your life, and He will fill your life with His presence and power.

Former Wheaton College president V. Raymond Edman said, "The Spirit-filled life is no mystery revealed to a select few, no goal difficult of attainment. To *trust* and *obey* is the substance of the whole matter."[5]

QUESTIONS

1. Describe in your own words the difference between the work of the Holy Spirit before and after Pentecost.
2. Why was it better for Jesus to ascend to heaven?
3. How would you show that the Holy Spirit is a person?
4. When does the Holy Spirit indwell a believer and for how long?
5. Why do believers in Christ still experience inner conflicts?
6. List a few things the Holy Spirit does for us.

NOTES

1. A. W. Tozer, *The Divine Conquest* (Old Tappan, N.J.: Revell, 1950), 66.

2. J. B. Phillips, *Letters to Young Churches* (New York: Macmillan, 1950), xiv.
3. G. Gampbell Morgan, *The Spirit of God* (New York: Revell, 1900), 93.
4. D. L. Moody, *New Sermons, Addresses and Prayers* (St. Louis: Thompsons, 1877).
5. *Draper's Book of Quotations* (Wheaton: Tyndale House, 1992), 315.

REMINDERS

"The world has yet to see what God can do with and for and through a man who is fully and wholly consecrated to Him." —*Henry Varley*

Pentecost marked the coming of the Spirit in a new way to live in the earthly bodies of all believers.

"The greatest miracle that God can do today is to take an unholy man out of an unholy world, and make that man holy, and put him back into that unholy world, and keep him holy in it!" —*Leonard Ravenhill*

"When we rely on organization, we get what organization can do. When we rely upon education, we get what education can do. When we rely on eloquence, we get what eloquence can do. But when we rely on the Holy Spirit, we get *what God can do.*" —A. C. Dixon

The secret of victory in your Christian life is the *indwelling Holy Spirit.* Allow Him to have undisputed control of your whole life.

Though we are not sinless, we should sin less, and less, and less.

"Therefore whoever hears these sayings of Mine, and does them, I will liken him to a wise man who built his house on the rock."

MATTHEW 7:24

"A man who loves his wife will love her letters and her photographs because they speak to him of her. So, if we love the Lord Jesus, we shall love the Bible because it speaks to us of him."

JOHN R. W. STOTT, AS QUOTED IN *DRAPER'S BOOK OF QUOTATIONS*

"Luther studied the Bible as one would gather apples: "First I shake the whole tree, that the ripest might fall. Then I climb the tree and shake each limb, and then each branch and then each twig, and then I look under each leaf."

"The Bible is the only thing that can combat the devil. Quote the Scriptures and the devil will run . . . use the Scriptures like a sword and you'll drive temptation away."

BILLY GRAHAM, AS QUOTED IN *DRAPER'S BOOK OF QUOTATIONS*

4

YOU AND YOUR BIBLE

THE BIBLE IS LITERALLY *God speaking to you.* It is God's instrument in salvation (Romans 10:17; 1 Peter 1:25) and God's instrument for growing, mature Christians (1 Peter 2:2). It is the blueprint for the Christian life.

The very first step in understanding the Bible is conversion. Paul said, "The natural man does *not* receive the things of the Spirit of God, for they are foolishness to him; nor can he know them, because they are spiritually discerned. But he who is spiritual judges all things, yet he himself is rightly judged by no one" (1 Corinthians 2:14–15).

The unsaved person can read the Bible and receive considerable inspiration, but the true Christian receives infinitely more. The gospel of John chapter 14, verse 26 tells us the Holy Spirit "will teach you" and "bring to your remembrance all things." To salvation must be added *submission*. The Bible must be read in a spirit of receptivity. This is the way to begin.

READ THE BIBLE PRAYERFULLY

Prayer is the "open sesame" to the Bible. Always begin your Bible reading with prayer for divine guidance. All of us in reading some current book have wished the author were present to answer and explain some things, but this is rarely possible. Amazing as it seems, though, this is possible when reading the Bible. James said, "If any of you lacks wisdom, let him ask of God, who gives to all liberally and without reproach, and it will be given to him" (James 1:5). God really wants to give us wisdom and understanding. The psalmist knew this truth, for centuries ago he prayed, "Open my eyes, that I may see wondrous things from Your law" (Psalm 119:18). It is really exciting to ask the Lord to show us some "wondrous things" each day out of His Word. After God does this for us, think about this truth, apply it, and put it to use.

John Newton said it this way: "By one hour's intimate access to the throne of grace, where the Lord causes His glory to pass before the soul that seeks Him, you may acquire more true spiritual knowledge and comfort than by a day's or a week's converse with the best of men, or the most studious perusal of many folios."[1]

The Bible is the result of men being moved by the Holy Spirit. In 2 Peter 1:21 we read, "For prophecy never came by the will of man, but holy men of God spoke as they were moved by the Holy Spirit." And again, "All Scripture is given by inspiration of God" (2 Timothy 3:16). The very same Holy Spirit who led these men to write longs to lead us today so we can understand. Without the Holy Spirit, the Bible is like an ocean that cannot be sounded, heavens that cannot be surveyed, mines that cannot be explored, and mysteries beyond unraveling. We must—we must—yield to the leadership of the Holy Spirit. Jesus said, "When He, the Spirit of truth, has come, He will *guide you into all truth*" (John 16:13). The Holy Spirit has come and dwells in every believer. Permit Him to guide you into God's truth. Without the illumination of the Holy Spirit, we read in vain. So read the Bible prayerfully.

READ THE BIBLE CAREFULLY

Of all the Christians at Berea, it was said, "These were more fair-minded than those in Thessalonica, in that they received the word with all readiness, and searched the Scriptures daily to find out whether these things were so" (Acts 17:11). The Bereans read the Scriptures carefully! Today the Bible is read a lot but studied little. To read with care requires concentration, so our minds must be alert. To read in a perfunctory way for the sake of conscience is not worth much.

Jesus said, "If anyone wills to do His will, he shall know concerning the doctrine, whether it is from God or whether I speak on My own authority" (John 7:17). This requires obedience. "If anyone wills to do His will, he shall know." All the icebergs of difficulty will melt before a ready and willing mind. Dark skies will be pierced, deep places fathomed, and wide rivers forded. Obedience to God's will results in an unshakable confidence in God's Word.

The Bereans also "searched the Scriptures daily." This requires work, for the great truths of God are not discovered by the casual reader. Diamonds are not found on the sidewalk. We must linger upon the Bible's chapters, verses, phrases, and words, eagerly seeking to understand its message. Yes, we must search like a miner looking for gold. The psalmist said, "Therefore I love Your commandments more than gold, yes, than fine gold!" (Psalm 119:127). We must search like a hungry man does for food. Jeremiah said, "Your words were found, and I ate them" (Jeremiah 15:16). Job said, "I have treasured the words of His mouth more than my necessary food" (Job 23:12). And again, "How sweet are

Your words to my taste, sweeter than honey to my mouth!" (Psalm 119:103). The little bee alights on the flower, then dips down to the very heart and sucks up the honey. Careful Bible reading will yield honey to the mouth. Jesus said, "You search the Scriptures, for in them you think you have eternal life" (John 5:39).

The Lord's formula for Joshua's success was: "This Book of the Law shall not depart out of your mouth, but you shall meditate in it day and night, that you may observe to do according to all that is written in it. For then you will make your way prosperous, and then you will have good success" (Joshua 1:8).

The word *meditate* means "to attend." All attention must be focused on the subject at hand. David's definition of a happy man in Psalm 1 is one whose "delight is in the law of the Lord." May God deliver us from a complacent, casual, cursory reading of the Word of God. Let us read the Bible carefully.

READ THE BIBLE SYSTEMATICALLY

First, let me suggest that you *set aside a definite time for Bible reading*, preferably at the beginning of the day when the mind is alert. At a prescribed time, in a quiet place, systematically read the Word of God.

Do not permit anything to interfere, no matter how

important it seems. Many well-meaning Christians who sincerely love the Lord are up and down in their Christian experience because they have no *definite time* with God. The old hymn states, "Take time to be holy, Speak oft with thy Lord." To this we could add *make time.* Beware of the barrenness of an overbusy life.

To read a portion of the Bible before retiring is fine but not sufficient. Not only should our last conscious thoughts be of the Lord but also our first thoughts. Give God the first part of the day, not the last; the best, not the worst. "But those who wait on the Lord shall renew their strength; they shall mount up with wings like eagles, they shall run and not be weary, they shall walk and not faint" (Isaiah 40:31).

Second, *begin at the beginning.* In reading any other book we start with chapter 1. To start a novel or biography in the middle results in confusion. The same holds true for the Bible. We cannot adequately understand Exodus apart from Genesis, or Hebrews apart from Leviticus. Too often we become so attached to certain favorite portions that we neglect the remainder of the Bible. Begin where God began, in Genesis, chapter 1, verse 1; and steadily go through to Revelation, chapter 22, verse 21.

Third, secure a notebook and *jot down some questions*, such as:

Who is speaking: God, an apostle, or the devil?
To whom was it written: saints or sinners?
What was the background of the writer and
    possibly the receiver?
What are the main ideas?
What seems to be the key verse?
What message is there for me today?

As you read, fill in the answers. Learn the facts, then apply them. This method of reading will help you grasp the entire book, thus avoiding error and misinterpretation. As you read, make sure you understand the words. If not, look them up. Get your bearings geographically and chronologically. Notice the marginal references and compare Scripture with Scripture.

Added to your regular reading, you might want to do some topical studying. This yields rich dividends. Take your concordance and look up the word *heaven*. Look up every passage in the Bible on this subject and record your findings. You will be thrilled at what you have learned.

Commentaries are helpful; however, beware of

being chained to them. Someone has humorously said, "The Bible throws a lot of light on the commentaries." Any book that takes priority over the Bible becomes a crutch that leads to weakness. To read the words of men and neglect the Word of God is to say that the books of men are of greater worth. Read the Bible systematically.

READ THE BIBLE TRUSTFULLY

Why? Because "without faith"—*without faith*—"it is impossible to please" God (Hebrews 11:6). Salvation, as well as Christian growth, depends on believing. Faith is necessary for understanding the Bible. That is exactly where Israel failed. "But the word which they heard did not profit them, not being mixed with faith in those who heard it" (Hebrews 4:2). We must—we must—believe God! We must read the Bible *trustfully.*

The Bible is living, not dead. If the Lord came personally to you, would you ignore Him? Well, God has spoken to you in the Bible! May we never neglect it. Just think of it! Not man's word but God's Word. May we sincerely say with Samuel, "Speak, Lord, for Your servant hears" (1 Samuel 3:9).

Imagine Mr. Jones at the close of a busy day. He is

weary in body and fatigued in mind. Just before going to bed he hurriedly reads one of the shorter psalms. Briefly he prays and falls into bed. Doubtless Mr. Jones will remember little of his reading. Every condition militates against it.

In contrast, picture Mr. Jones at the beginning of the day. He is rested in body and ready in mind. In a definite place at a definite time, he starts the day with God. After prayer for the Spirit's guidance, he reads with care, answering obvious questions and making brief notations of his findings. Occasionally a verse must be looked up or a passage of Scripture compared with another. After systematic study he is ready for all the events of the day. The Word of God will protect him against evil. His new spiritual discoveries may be applied and put to use. We can be reasonably sure he will "grow in the grace and knowledge of our Lord and Savior Jesus Christ" (2 Peter 3:18).

To grow in the things of God, we should read the Bible *prayerfully, carefully, systematically,* and, most of all, *trustfully.* "The Holy Scriptures tell us what we could never learn any other way: They tell us what we are, who we are, how we got here, why we are here, and what we are required to do while we remain here."[2]

QUESTIONS

1. List two verses of Scripture that indicate the Bible is God's instrument in salvation and Christian growth.
2. Why is conversion the first step in understanding the Bible?
3. In what way is prayer related to an understanding of Scripture? (Psalm 119:18).
4. In what way were the Christians at Berea examples to us today? (Acts 17:11).
5. List three ways in which a Christian should read his Bible.
6. Why is it vital to read the Bible trustfully?

NOTES

1. John Newton, *The Works of the Reverend John Newton* (Henry G. Bohn, 1871), 120.
2. A. W. Tozer, *Of God and Men* (Harrisburg, Pa.: Christian Pubns., n.d.), 30.

REMINDERS

The very first step in understanding the Bible is *conversion.*

"The Bible is a letter from God with our personal address on it." —Søren A. Kierkegaard, as quoted in *Draper's Book of Quotations*

John Newton said, "By one hour's intimate access to the throne of grace, where the Lord causes His glory to pass before the soul that seeks Him, you may acquire more true spiritual knowledge and comfort than by a day's or a week's converse with the best of men, or the most studious perusal of many folios."

The same Holy Spirit who led these men to write, longs to lead us today so we can understand.

The Bereans "searched the Scriptures daily" (Acts 17:11). This requires work, for the great truths of God are not discovered by the casual reader. Diamonds are not found on the sidewalk.

"The Bible that's falling apart probably belongs to someone . . . who isn't." —Christina Johnson, as quoted in *Draper's Book of Quotations*

"Ask, and it will be given to you;
seek, and you will find; knock,
and it will be opened to you."

MATTHEW 7:7

"Pray for great things, expect great things,
work for great things, but above all, pray."

R. A. TORREY

Prayer is the key that unlocks
the door to God's treasures.

"To become accomplished in anything, you
must practice. If you want to learn to pray,
then pray—again and again and again."

R. C. SPROUL, *Following Christ*,
TYNDALE HOUSE 1984

5

HOW TO PRAY

THE DISCIPLES CAME TO JESUS one day and asked, "Lord, teach us to pray" (Luke 11:1). They had noticed that no one ever prayed like Jesus, and as they watched and listened to the prayers of Jesus, they realized their own desperate need. They did not ask "Lord, teach us to preach" but "Teach us to pray."

At first, prayer may be awkward. The words may come slowly, but keep on praying, for through prayer we can enter into the very presence of God. We can make our needs known to Him, but, greater still, we can worship and commune with God.

WHAT IS PRAYER?

The dictionary describes prayer as a reverent or devout petition to God, an entreaty. Certainly prayer is that. The simplest definition of prayer is the three letter word *cry*. In Romans 8:15, Paul says, "For you did not receive the spirit of bondage again to fear, but you received the Spirit of adoption by whom we *cry* out, 'Abba, Father.'"

Prayer is a cry. When we pray, we are crying out to God. "Lord, help me." "Lord, give me wisdom." "Lord, reveal Yourself to me." Prayer is a cry. Just as a little child cries to his parent, we cry to God.

A. W. Tozer reminds us, "When Peter was starting to sink under those waters of Galilee, he had no time to consult the margin of someone's Bible to find out how he should pray. He just prayed out of his heart and out of his desperation, 'Lord, save me!'"[1]

But *prayer is also a call.* In Jeremiah 33:3, Jehovah's words are "Call to Me, and I will answer you, and show you great and mighty things, which you do not know."

Prayer is asking. Again, our Lord said in Luke 11:9, "Ask, and it will be given to you; seek, and you will find; knock, and it will be opened to you."

But *prayer is also communion.* "How rare it is," said Fenelon, "to find a soul quiet enough to hear God speak." Prayer is talking to God and having Him talk to us. It is spending time in communion with our heavenly Father.

One day the five-year-old son of D. L. Moody went into the study where his father sat writing.

Wanting no interruptions, Mr. Moody gruffly asked, "Well, what do you want?"

"Nothing, Daddy," the boy replied. "I just wanted to be where you are." Sitting on the floor, he began to amuse himself quietly. He desired only companion-ship.

G. Campbell Morgan, the gifted English preacher, relates that it was "this little incident, told by Mr. Moody, that helped me greatly to understand the true meaning of prayer. To pray is to be where Jesus is. When we are in His presence, we need nothing more to pray prevailingly."

WHY SHOULD WE PRAY?

The answer to why we should pray is very simple: the Bible tells us to pray. In Luke 18:1, Jesus said that we should pray and not lose heart. Prayer is God's cure for caving in. In Matthew 9:38 we are admon-ished to pray that the Lord of the harvest will send forth laborers into His harvest.

Why pray? The answer is, *because Jesus prayed.* His entire life on earth was an example of prayer.

Since Jesus Christ, the sinless Son of God, found prayer important, we sinful creatures find prayer indispensable! Jesus prayed at the beginning of His public ministry when He was baptized: "When all the people were baptized, it came to pass that Jesus also was baptized; and while He prayed, the heaven was opened" (Luke 3:21).

Before choosing the twelve apostles, He spent all night in prayer: "Now it came to pass in those days that He went out to the mountain to pray, and continued all night in prayer to God. And when it was day, He called His disciples to Himself; and from them He chose twelve whom He also named apostles" (Luke 6:12–13).

He prayed before feeding the five thousand: "And Jesus took the loaves, and when He had given thanks He distributed them to the disciples, and the disciples to those sitting down; and likewise of the fish, as much as they wanted" (John 6:11). Jesus prayed before rescuing the disciples at sea. The Bible says, "He went up on the mountain by Himself to pray" (Matthew 14:23).

At the grave of Lazarus, He prayed: "Then they took away the stone from the place where the dead man was lying. And Jesus lifted up His eyes and said, "Father, I thank You that You have heard Me" (John 11:41).

At the Last Supper, Jesus prayed: "And as they

were eating, Jesus took bread, blessed it and broke it, and gave it to them and said, 'Take, eat; this is My body'" (Mark 14:22).

In Gethsemane, Jesus agonized in prayer (Matthew 26:36–44). Our Lord prayed often, and so must each Christian learn to pray.

Why pray? *Because Jesus Christ is praying for us—right now.* The Bible says, "He always lives to make intercession for them" (Hebrews 7:25).

Why pray? *Because prayer is the example given to us by the early church.* Of the apostolic church we read, "And they continued steadfastly in the apostles' doctrine and fellowship, in the breaking of bread, and in prayers" (Acts 2:42).

Before the day of Pentecost, they gathered together to pray: "These all continued with one accord in prayer and supplication, with the women and Mary the mother of Jesus, and with His brothers" (Acts 1:14). After Pentecost they "joined together constantly" in prayer.

When Peter was jailed, they prayed until God delivered him: "So, when he had considered this, he came to the house of Mary, the mother of John whose surname was Mark, where many were gathered together praying" (Acts 12:12).

The apostolic church saturated their efforts with prayer. The apostle James told the Christians of his time that their spiritual poverty was due to neglect of prayer: "You do not have because you do not ask" (James 4:2).

HOW SHOULD WE PRAY?

1. *We should pray humbly.* The apostle James tells us that "God resists the proud, but gives grace to the humble" (4:6). Have you ever had anyone resist you? At every opportunity they fought you; they were totally disagreeable. That is a difficult situation to be in. But there is nothing—absolutely nothing—so hopeless as having God resist you.

R. C. Sproul has well said, "Prayer has a vital place in the life of the Christian. First, it is an absolute prerequisite for salvation. Some people cannot hear; yet though deaf, they can be saved. Some may not be able to see; yet though blind, they can be saved. Knowledge of the Good News—salvation through the atoning death and resurrection of Jesus Christ—will come from one source or another, but in the final analysis a person must humbly ask God for salvation. The prayer of salvation is the one prayer of the wicked, God has said he will hear."[2]

2. *We should pray specifically.* Robert Cook, former pastor and youth leader, tells of a missionary who was evacuated during World War II from a South Pacific island. He was put on a freighter that zigzagged through enemy waters in its journey to safety. One day, right before the ship, there appeared the periscope of an enemy submarine.

"That's when I learned to pray specifically," said the missionary. "While the enemy was looking our ship over (probably trying to decide whether or not to sink us) we prayed over every inch of that sub. 'Lord, stop his motors!' 'Jam his torpedo tubes!' 'Break his rudder!'"[3]

That missionary prayed specifically. Why? Because he had a specific need—his life was in danger.

Our prayers don't need to be long. Many of our Lord's prayers were only a few words. The important thing is that they be specific.

3. *We should pray believingly.* General Booth, founder of the Salvation Army, advised people to "work as if everything depended upon your work, and pray as if everything depended upon your prayer."

Pray—expecting God to answer! In Hebrews 11:6 we are told that "without faith it is impossible to please Him, for he who comes to God must believe that He is, and that He is a rewarder of those who diligently seek Him."

James says, "But let him ask in faith, with no doubting, for he who doubts is like a wave of the sea driven and tossed by the wind. For let not that man suppose that he will receive anything from the Lord" (James 1:6–7).

It was said of Praying Hyde, missionary to India, "He prayed as if God were at his elbow, standing ready to answer. He had faith."

> Without faith—we cannot be saved.
> Without faith—we cannot grow.
> Without faith—we cannot please God.
> Without faith—we will have no answer to our prayers.
> Pray believingly!

4. *We should pray intelligently.* Ideally, our prayers should include the four areas of adoration, confession, thanksgiving, and supplication. As we review God's attributes, we see our human weaknesses,

which leads us to earnest confession. Thankfulness naturally follows, leading us to supplication.

When I consult my doctor or lawyer, I carefully prepare my thoughts and questions to maximize my opportunity. When we talk to God, we should intelligently bring our requests and petitions before Him. Again James says, "You ask and do not receive, because you ask amiss, that you may spend it on your pleasures" (James 4:3). That brings me to another important point. We need to ask ourselves, "Can God grant my request?" For example, you should not pray, "Lord, make my husband become a Christian." God doesn't work that way. You ought rather to pray, "Lord, help me to lovingly relate the gospel to my husband so he might accept You as his Savior."

We also need to ask, "Have I done my part? Am I setting the proper example? Am I demonstrating Christ's love in my life?"

If a man prays for God to give him a job, he must be willing to read the want ads. The Lord always expects us to do our part in prayer.

5. *We should pray obediently.* There is no way we can be successful in our prayer life if we are living with unconfessed sin. The psalmist declared, "If I regard iniquity in my heart, the Lord will not hear"

(Psalm 66:18). Sin—unconfessed sin—is disobedience. Sin blocks our communication with God. It knocks down the power lines.

"A man may engage in a great deal of humble talk before God and get no response because unknown to himself he is using prayer to disguise disobedience."[4] Jesus said, "If you love Me, keep My commandments" (John 14:15). We need to pray to God from an obedient heart.

WHEN SHOULD WE PRAY?

It would be difficult to pray in the wrong place or at the wrong time. Jonah prayed powerfully in the belly of the fish. Paul and Silas prayed at midnight in the dungeon.

We can pray anytime, anywhere. However, it is best to have a definite time and place for daily prayer. David said, "Evening and morning and at noon I will pray, and cry aloud, and He shall hear my voice" (Psalm 55:17).

Of Daniel we read, "Now when Daniel knew that the writing was signed, he went home. And in his upper room, with his windows open toward Jerusalem, he knelt down on his knees three times that day, and prayed and gave thanks before his God, as was his custom since early days" (Daniel 6:10).

Jesus had told us to enter into the private place to pray: "But you, when you pray, go into your room, and when you have shut your door, pray to your Father who is in the secret place; and your Father who sees in secret will reward you openly" (Matthew 6:6).

Whenever God's people gather, whether to eat, to study the Bible, or to socialize, it is right to pray, asking God's blessing.

Do not forget the need for family prayer, a practice that draws the family together with a common cord.

FOR WHAT SHALL WE PRAY?

We are to pray for all things needful for our physical and spiritual welfare. "If you then, being evil, know how to give good gifts to your children, how much more will your Father who is in heaven give good things to those who ask Him!" (Matthew 7:11).

Jesus taught His disciples to pray for their daily bread. This infers the needs of life: food, clothing, and shelter. Nothing is too large or too small for God. We are invited to take everything to God in prayer.

OBSTACLES TO PRAYER

Prayer is not easy; it is difficult. Unbelief, worldliness, and indifference render prayer useless.

Consider the following Bible verses:

"Behold, the Lord's hand is not shortened, that it cannot save; nor His ear heavy, that it cannot hear. But your iniquities have separated you from your God; and your sins have hidden His face from you, so that He will not hear" (Isaiah 59:1–2).

"If I regard iniquity in my heart, the Lord will not hear" (Psalm 66:18).

"For the eyes of the Lord are on the righteous, and His ears are open to their prayers; but the face of the Lord is against those who do evil" (1 Peter 3:12).

Sin causes mankind to be lost, and sin in the believer's life makes prayer worthless. Thus it forms a vicious cycle. Ask God to keep you from sin.

Prayer is a gracious privilege. It is a glorious calling. It is the key that opens the door to knowing God in all His holiness and omnipotence. I urge you to cultivate prayer.

QUESTIONS

1. Give two biblical definitions of prayer as found in Romans 8:15 and Jeremiah 33:3.
2. List at least three reasons why we should pray, and verify these with Scripture.
3. List five areas of concern under the heading "How Should I Pray?"
4. According to James 1:6–7, what is a key element in prayer?
5. What are some general areas of prayer?
6. List some obstacles to prayer and the solution.

NOTES

1. A. W. Tozer, *Who Put Jesus on the Cross* (Harrisburg, Pa.: Christian Pubns., 1976), 103.
2. R. C. Sproul, *Following Christ* (Wheaton: Tyndale House, 1984), 107–8.
3. Robert Cook, *Walk with the King Today* (Chappaqua, N.Y.: Christian Herald, 1978), 26.
4. A. W. Tozer, *Man: The Dwelling Place of God* (Harrisburg, Pa.: Christian Pubns, n.d.), 90.

REMINDERS

Prayer is the key that unlocks the door to God's treasures.

The simplest definition of prayer is the three-letter word *cry.*

The first key to fruitful praying is a spirit of humility.

General William Booth said, "Work as if everything depended upon your work, and pray as if everything depended upon your prayer."

Sin blocks our communication with God. It knocks down the power lines.

Prayer is not only our privilege, but it is our duty. Neglect of prayer is disobedience, which displeases God.

"Prayer is the gymnasium of the soul." (Missionary Samuel Zwemer)

"Good morning, God, I love you! What are you up to today? I want to be part of it." —Missionary Norman Grubb

"Now in the morning, having risen
a long while before daylight,
He went out and departed to a
solitary place; and there He prayed."

MARK 1:35

Andrew Bonar, a servant of God,
had three rules that he lived by:
Rule 1 — Not to speak to any person before
speaking to Jesus Christ.
Rule 2 — Not to do anything with his hands
until he had been on his knees.
Rule 3 — Not to read the papers until he had
read his Bible.

6

DAILY PRAYER AND BIBLE STUDY

WE LIVE IN A FAST-MOVING, noisy world! The pace at which many of us operate is frightening. More than ever before, we need to budget our time to do those things that must be done. Because of our hectic schedules, many important activities get lost in the shuffle. They're left undone.

We must each decide what our priorities will be. We alone determine what will come first in our lives. Whether to spend time talking with God or to spend time doing something else is a decision each of us must make. We must decide what is primary and what is secondary.

Unfortunately, for many Christians, *a daily time of prayer and Bible reading* does not rank high enough on the list. It becomes a casualty to the clock. It is often left out of our day. The activity that should be most important to us is put aside, leaving us spiritually unprepared for the battles of daily living. This time given to prayer and Bible reading is often referred to as "daily devotions," "the morning watch," or "a quiet time."

WHAT IS "THE QUIET TIME"?

The Christian's quiet time is the time one spends sharing with God the Father. It is, more specifically, the definite time set aside each day for prayer, meditation, and the study of God's Word. It is from this quiet time with God that we derive strength, wisdom, and guidance for each day. Without a daily devotional life, we remain spiritually anemic, hungry, and an easy prey to the devil.

The quiet time is like a spiritual shower or bath. It washes, refreshes, and revives us. It helps protect us from the moral corruption around us. It prepares us, as Christian soldiers, to engage in spiritual warfare.

Yes, my friend, the daily devotional life of the believer is an indispensable ingredient for a successful Christian life. Jesus said, "It is written, 'Man shall not live by bread alone, but by every word that proceeds from the mouth of God'" (Matthew 4:4).

John R. W. Stott, in his book *Basic Christianity*, says it well:

Our relationship to our heavenly Father, though secure, is not static. He ardently desires that His children shall grow up to know Him more and more intimately. Generations of Christians have discovered that the only way to do so is to make time to wait upon Him every day. What many people call the daily "quiet times," first thing in the morning and last thing at night, are an indispensable necessity for the Christian who wants to make progress.[1]

The Christian knows Jesus Christ as his Savior; but unless he spends regular periods in quietness and meditation in the Word of God, he will never know Jesus better.

Louis Smith writes of a woman who had been a Christian for many years. And yet, because of tension and emptiness in her life, she was on the verge of a nervous collapse. As she prayed to the Lord for help, the Holy Spirit directed her to a verse in Isaiah 30 that she had never noticed before. It was verse 15, where the Bible declares, "in quietness and confidence shall be your strength."

The woman began using half an hour before her family woke up for her quiet time. She began to read

God's Word and to consciously consider the love, greatness, and power of God. One morning, on a day that was to be filled with several difficult commitments, she was considering the children of Israel as they crossed the Red Sea. "When I realized how easily God took several million people through that sea," the lady commented, "I knew He could take me safely through any Red Sea that might arise in my day. I left my quiet time with assurance, confidence, and faith."

Within a short while the woman's nervousness had completely vanished. She soon became such a bulwark of inspiration and strength that people could not believe she had ever been threatened by a nervous breakdown.[2]

Christians today are bombarded by distractions. I am sure Satan uses everything he can to keep us from simply being quiet before God. Noise pollution takes its toll on all of us. Radios and televisions blare all day long. Telephones ring incessantly. Automobiles and airplanes, machinery of every kind, make us almost numb to the beauty of quietness.

Our mechanized society, with all its labor-saving devices, has actually become more hectic than ever. We are caught up, it seems, in one continuous flurry of activity. And when we finally do set aside a few moments for devotions, we find that our minds are filled with a hundred-and-one people to see, things to do, and places to go.

And so many Christians go on and on, never seeming to find time to spend with God and, as a result, rarely enjoying the fruitful, abundant life that Christ offers to us.

The quiet time is not just a helpful idea; it is absolutely necessary for spiritual growth. Just as it is easier to fight off a cold if we are in good physical condition, so it is easier to fight off evil if we are spiritually fit.

So—no matter who you are—new Christian, old Christian, pastor or layman—you have little hope of living triumphantly unless you seriously cultivate your quiet time. Isaiah wrote, "Even the youths shall faint and be weary, and the young men shall utterly fall, but those who wait on the Lord shall renew their strength; they shall mount up with wings like eagles, they shall run and not be weary, they shall walk and not faint" (Isaiah 40:30–31).

"All right," you say, "I agree that the quiet time is important, but I have never been successful in keeping one. It doesn't seem to work for me."

HELPFUL SUGGESTIONS

How can we "be still" and know God in the midst of this high-pressure society? How can we encourage a successful quiet time? Here are some suggestions I have found helpful in my personal life.

1. *Recognize the importance of a quiet time.* It is easy to give lip service to our need for fellowship with God. It is another thing entirely to be personally committed to those words. We are never truly successful at what we do unless we are committed to its achievement.

Jack Wyrtzen, evangelist and founder of Word of Life Fellowship, continually challenged me to cultivate a daily quiet time. His daily Bible reading became *the theme* of his day. Jack often said that his daily quiet time was *his lifeline.*

Peter wrote, "As newborn babes, desire the pure milk of the word, that you may grow thereby" (1 Peter 2:2).

Martin Luther said that "to be a Christian without prayer is no more possible than to be alive without breathing." Communication with Jesus Christ through prayer and through His Word is the spiritual lifeline of every believer.

Jesus Himself spent much time in meditation and prayer. Mark 1:35 reads, "Now in the morning, having risen a long while before daylight, He went out and departed to a solitary place; and there He prayed." If Jesus Christ, who was in perfect harmony with God the Father, withdrew to a solitary place for prayer, how can we do less?

2. *Cultivate a taste for the quiet time.* Peter challenges us to "desire" the Word of God (1 Peter 2:2). Jeremiah wrote, "Your words were found, and I ate them, and Your word was to me the joy and rejoicing of my heart" (Jeremiah 15:16).

"How do you eat the Word?" you ask. Well, what happens when you take physical food into your body? That glass of white milk you drink turns into blue eyes and blonde hair. Those green vegetables you eat become a part of your brown or yellow or white skin. What you digest becomes a part of you.

So the same is to be true as we read and meditate upon God's Word. We are to digest it. It is to become a part of our lives.

We should also desire to talk with God, to share with Him in prayer. Because I love my wife, I want to be with her. I enjoy talking to her. When I am traveling away from home, I eagerly look forward to calling her on the phone.

If we sincerely love Jesus Christ, we should have

this same desire. We will want to be in contact with Him. For you and me to have fellowship with God is an awesome thing. But even more wonderful is the realization that almighty God seeks our fellowship. John writes that "the Father is seeking such to worship Him" (John 4:23). Just think of it, God desires to meet with me! My quiet time is my time alone with God.

3. *Determine to maintain the quiet time.* The maintenance of a successful quiet time requires determination and discipline. Seek to avoid interruptions. Don't let the telephone rob you of your time with God. Arrange your schedule, if possible, so that you can be alone—totally alone—with God for a specific length of time each day.

"But you don't know my schedule," you say. "You don't know how busy I am."

If you are too busy to maintain a quiet time, I'm afraid you are too busy. I have found that we have time for just about anything that is really important to us. *We do what we want to do.*

What's important to you? If you want to look attractive, you spend the necessary time in front of the mirror. If you enjoy reading, you are likely to spend several hours per day with a book. Civic work, even church work, takes up our time because we are convinced of its importance.

But what about fellowship with God? If we don't maintain a quiet time each day, it's not because we are too busy; it's because we do not feel it is important enough.

It is said that John Wesley preached more than 44,000 sermons in his lifetime. He traveled by horseback and carriage nearly 30,000 miles, wrote grammar and theological textbooks in four languages, and yet always had time for a quiet time. While still in his childhood, Wesley resolved to dedicate an hour each morning and evening to Bible study and prayer.

Maintaining a daily quiet time is basically a matter of putting first things first. Dorothy Haskin tells the story of a noted concert artist who was asked the secret of her mastery of the violin. "Planned neglect," she replied. Then she explained: "There were many things that used to demand my time. When I went to my room after breakfast, I made my bed, straightened the room, dusted, and did whatever seemed necessary. When I finished my work, I turned to my violin practice. That system failed, however, to accomplish what I should on the violin, so I reversed things. I deliberately planned to neglect everything else until my practice period was complete. And that program of planned neglect is the secret of my success."

Perhaps there are some things you need to neglect so that you can be successful in maintaining your time with God. We must make time for fellowship with our heavenly Father. We organize for everything else, so why not organize for a quiet time?

"Prayer is the key of the morning and the bolt of the evening," said Matthew Henry. Discipline is required for a faithful, fruitful quiet time.

PRACTICAL STEPS IN DEVELOPING THE QUIET TIME

1. *Be regular.* The Christians in the city of Berea "searched the Scriptures daily" (Acts 17:11).

Seek to meet the Lord at the same time and same place each day. A *definite time and place* will help a great deal in developing regularity.

Do not attempt to bite off more than you can chew to begin with. To attempt too much to start with can lead to discouragement and failure. It is also wiser to begin with fifteen minutes daily than a few hours once a week. Determine to do only that which you honestly feel you can accomplish each day.

2. *Be quiet.* "In quietness and confidence shall be your strength" (Isaiah 30:15).

Make your quiet time a *quiet* time. "Be still, and know that I am God" (Psalm 46:10). There's an old navy rule: when ships readjust their compass, they drop anchor in a quiet spot. Decide where you can find a quiet spot. If you cannot find a quiet place, then you will have to close the door of your mind to all the surrounding distractions.

More important than finding a quiet spot is a quiet spirit. Open yourself to all that God has for you. While a student at the Moody Bible Institute, I was introduced to William Runyan's hymn, "Lord, I Have Shut the Door."

> Lord, I have shut the door,
> Speak now the word
> Which in the din and throng
> Could not be heard;
> Hushed now my inner heart,
> Whisper Thy will,
> While I have come apart,
> While all is still.

3. *Be systematic.* "They received the word with all readiness" (Acts 17:11).

The time you choose for your quiet time is up to you.

Missionary Hudson Taylor used to say, "Whatever is your best time in the day, give that to communion with God." Some people wake up quickly while others wake up slowly. Some of us are roosters and others are owls.

Consistency is the important thing. I have personally found the morning to be the best time for my quiet time with God. The psalmist wrote, "My voice You shall hear in the morning, O Lord; in the morning I will direct it to You, and I will look up" (Psalm 5:3). The Lord said, "I love those who love me, and those who seek me diligently will find me" (Proverbs 8:17).

If you are like most people, you are probably more alert in the morning than you are just before bedtime. But in order to regularly meet God in the morning, you must get to bed at a reasonable time. You may have to set your priorities in order. You may have to put that book or magazine down a little earlier. You may have to switch off the TV or radio.

Consistency requires faithfulness. The apostle Paul wrote, "Moreover is it required in stewards that one be found faithful" (1 Corinthians 4:2). Each one of us is a steward. We have twenty-four hours in every day to spend as we wish. How are you using your time?

When a person receives Jesus Christ as Savior, he becomes a member of the family of God. God becomes our heavenly Father, and we become His children. This is how we really get to know each other.

I would suggest that the quiet time begin with prayer to God, worshiping, confessing, and asking for His blessing on your time together. Prayer is the key that unlocks the treasures of God's Word.

Prayer time should include praise and thanksgiving for all God is doing and will do. Pray for your loved ones. Pray for others. Pray for yourself. It is a thrilling privilege to pray.

After prayer, you'll want to read God's Word, His special message to you. Secure a rather large Bible with print that is easy to read. Small type can be discouraging.

To meditate is to think quietly and deeply about the greatness and goodness of God. Notice the promises of God. Look for guiding principles for your daily life. Commit to memory a meaningful verse. Don't hurry. Regularly, quietly, systematically, yet leisurely, meditate upon the written Word and the living Word.

4. *Be rested.* "I will give you rest" (Exodus 33:14).

Spiritual rest is a gift from God. However, it is extremely important that we enjoy physical rest. It is difficult physically to get to bed late and get up early. Late nights can kill the quiet time.

5. *Be expectant.* "Now to Him who is able to do exceedingly abundantly above all that we ask or think, according to the power that works in us" (Ephesians 3:20).

Remember that in order to have a successful quiet time, you must expect God to do something for you each day. Pray expecting Him to answer your prayers. Ask Him to open your mind and heart to His fullness. Read His Word, expecting Him to speak to you to meet a specific need in your life.

Do you lack power in your life? Does it feel as if there is something missing in your Christian experience? Why not purpose in your heart from this day forward that you will develop your quiet time.

QUESTIONS

1. What is the quiet time?
2. According to Mark 1:35, what was the example of Jesus in the quiet time?
3. How would you relate Jeremiah 15:16 to a quiet time?
4. What part does discipline play in cultivating the quiet time?
5. List some practical steps in developing the quiet time.

NOTES

1. John R. W. Stott, *Basic Christianity,* 2d ed. (Grand Rapids: Eerdmans, 1958).
2. Louise Smith, "Be Still and Know God," *Christian Life* (May 1961): 30.

REMINDERS

The quiet time is not just a helpful idea; it is absolutely necessary to spiritual growth.

Martin Luther said, "To be a Christian without prayer is no more possible than to be alive without breathing."

If we don't maintain a quiet time each day, it's not because we are too busy; it's because we do not feel it is important enough.

There's an old navy rule: when ships readjust their compass, they drop anchor in a quiet spot.

Late nights can kill the quiet time.

"But the natural man does not receive the things of the Spirit of God, for they are foolishness to him; nor can he know them, because they are spiritually discerned. But he who is spiritual judges all things, yet he himself is rightly judged by no one."

1 Corinthians 2:14–15

"We may take comfort about our souls if we know anything of an inward fight and conflict. It is the invariable companion of genuine Christian holiness . . . Do we find in our heart of hearts a spiritual struggle? Do we feel anything of the flesh lusting against the Spirit and the Spirit against the flesh, so that we cannot do the things that we would? Are we conscious of two principles within us, contending for the mastery? Do we feel anything of war in our inward man? Well, let us thank God for it! It is a good sign. It is strongly probably evidence of the great work of sanctification . . . Anything is better than apathy, stagnation, deadness and indifference."

J. C. Ryle, *Holiness*

7

DIVISIONS
OF MANKIND

OUR WORLD IS DIVIDED by wealth, education, race, age, and even geography. Some of these divisions are natural and helpful. Others are artificial and harmful.

The Bible divides all of mankind into two major groups. These divisions are not according to the measure of our possessions or the color of our skin. In fact, the apostle Paul tells us that in Christ there is "Neither Jew nor Greek . . . slave nor free . . . male nor female" (Galatians 3:28).

God's divisions of mankind are based entirely upon the *spiritual condition* of the human heart! In the New Testament book of 1 Corinthians 2:14–3:4, Paul talks about these divisions of mankind.

THE NATURAL MAN

The first division described is that of the natural man. In 1 Corinthians 2:14 we read that "the natural man does not receive the things of the Spirit of God, for they are foolishness to him; nor can he know them, because they are spiritually discerned."

Who is the natural man? He is the person who has been born *only once.* He is alive physically but dead spiritually. He is motivated primarily by his own physical desires. He is unbelieving, unconverted, and unsaved.

Once a religious leader named Nicodemus came to Jesus seeking spiritual guidance. Jesus told him that "unless one is born of water and the Spirit, he cannot enter the kingdom of God" (John 3:5). Jesus then defined the natural man. "That which is born of the flesh is flesh" (v. 6). The natural man is flesh. Jesus Christ is not in the life. Self is supreme. Jesus Christ is excluded.

The natural man is, for the most part, ego centered. He basically functions and seeks his fulfillment in the human senses.

Although he may be outwardly gracious, courteous, and kind, he is inwardly self-centered and seeks primarily to gratify his fleshly desires. His spirit has never been touched by the Holy Spirit, and he is separated from God.

Despite natural gifts and physical accomplishments, the natural man experiences a major void in his life. It was Pascal who declared, "There is a God-shaped vacuum in every heart," and we know that only God can fill that void. Henry Thoreau, the naturalist author, confessed, "The mass of men live lives in quiet desperation!"

The first great division of mankind is "the natural man." To the natural man the things of God are foreign. Paul tells us that he is unable to comprehend the things of God; he can't tune in because he has no aptitude for measuring diving truth. The natural man is on a different wavelength and operates on a different level.

The Bible goes on to tell us that the natural man does not understand the things of God. Why? Because "they are foolishness to him" (1 Corinthians 2:14). The word *foolish* comes from the Greek adjective *moros,* meaning dull, tasteless, and insipid. In other words, spiritual matters are distasteful and may even seem moronic to the man without Christ. Not only are the things of God foolishness to the natural man, but the Scripture continues, "nor can he know them" (v. 14). It is not just that he does not know; he *cannot* know the things of God because "they are spiritually discerned" (v. 14).

A young college professor once said to me, "I've tried to read the Bible a hundred times. It just doesn't add up. I was reared in a good home. I even have a brother who is a minister; but for some reason, I just can't seem to understand it."

My friend, this is no mystery. Paul said, "Nor can he know them" because "they are spiritually discerned" (1 Corinthians 2:14).

THE SPIRITUAL MAN

In 1 Corinthians 2:15–16, Paul speaks of the second division of mankind. Here he presents a picture of the spiritual man. "He who is spiritual," says Paul, "judges all things, yet he himself is rightly judged by no one. For 'who has known the mind of the Lord that he may instruct Him?' But we have the mind of Christ."

Who is the spiritual man? Paul is not speaking of the rank and file of believers. The spiritual man is certainly a believer, but more than that, he is one whose life is guided by the Holy Spirit of God. Jesus Christ is not only in his life, but He is in charge of his life. He has experienced the second birth, and Jesus Christ is Lord. Jesus Christ reigns and rules.

The apostle Paul was a spiritual man. To the

believers of Galatia, he wrote, "I have been crucified with Christ; it is no longer I who live, but Christ lives in me; and the life which I now live in the flesh I live by faith in the Son of God" (Galatians 2:20).

The spiritual man is the person who has committed himself to Christ. Jesus Christ is supreme in his life. In contrast to the immaturity of the carnal person, the spiritual person is one who grows in the things of God and brings forth fruit. The spiritual man is one who has experienced the love of God and who in turn is desirous of sharing that love with others.

The natural man *does not know God.* The carnal person *does not recognize the supremacy of Christ.* It is the spiritual man who is motivated and directed by the constraining love of Christ and the indwelling Holy Spirit.

According to 1 Corinthians 2:15, we find that the spiritual man is given *discernment.* The spiritual man is able to make right decisions, understand the Scriptures, and live in God's perfect will.

Finally, the spiritual man is one who displays *the mind of Christ.* Paul instructed believers at Philippi: "Let this mind be in you which was also in Christ Jesus" (Philippians 2:5). The spiritual man is characterized by the mind of Christ, a mind of service and submission.

He displays the mind of one who "made Himself of no reputation, taking the form of a bondservant . . . [who] humbled Himself and became obedient to the point of death, even the death of the cross" (vv. 7–8).

Following Paul's presentation of the natural man and the spiritual man, he writes about carnality in the Corinthian church (1 Corinthians 3:1–9). Paul says in verse 1, "I, brethren, could not speak to you as to spiritual men, but as to men of the flesh, as to infants in Christ" (NASB). That condition *continued*, so that after a considerable period of time, Paul writes in verse 3, "for you are *still* fleshly."

Now, of course, there is nothing wrong with being a spiritual baby. That's where *we all begin*. Peter, speaking to new Christians, writes, "As newborn babes, desire the pure milk of the word" (1 Peter 2:2). We all start our Christian experience as infants—as newborn babies.

But the tragedy occurs when a person *remains* a baby Christian. A mother is understandably alarmed if her baby fails to develop normally. A farmer is financially ruined if his crops do not grow and bring forth fruit. The first law of life is growth. Without growth, there can be no future development!

Why is it important that we grow as Christians?

Because it is God's purpose for us. In Romans 8:29 we read "whom He foreknew, He also predestined to be conformed to the image of His Son." God desires that we become like Jesus Christ. Frustrated and unfulfilled is the Christian who resists God's design for development.

Look for a moment at the characteristics of the carnal person. Like an infant, he is easily offended and hurt. A small baby will cry at the slightest provocation. Any unusual activity is likely to disturb him. The carnal Christian is shortsighted. As with the young child, he lacks judgment and is immature. As these characteristics are normal for the child, they are also normal for the young Christian. It is only as the Christian *fails to mature* that carnality expresses itself. Unfortunately, many Christians remain spiritual infants throughout their lifetime. Their growth has been arrested.

Envy, strife, and divisions are characteristics of the carnal person. In 1 Corinthians 3:3 Paul says, "For where there are envy, strife, and divisions among you, are you not carnal and behaving like mere men?" Children often quarrel and fight. They are impatient and lack self-control. Many times they are unable to get along with one another.

It was carnal Christians who caused many of the problems in the New Testament church. Much of Paul's time and many of his letters were devoted to resolving the strife created by carnal believers.

Why? Because although Jesus Christ was in their lives, He was not supreme. They were more concerned with the physical than they were with the spiritual issues of life.

My friend, where do you stand today? Are you growing? Is your spiritual life fruitful or unfruitful? Are you a carnal Christian—"saved yet so as by fire"?

In an Italian city stands a statue of a Grecian maiden with a beautiful face, graceful figure, and noble expression. One day a poor peasant girl came face-to-face with the statue. She stood and stared, and then went home to wash her face and comb her hair. The next day she came again to stand before the statue and then returned home once more. This time she mended her tattered clothing. Day by day, as she gazed at the statue, *she changed*. Her form grew more graceful and her face more refined, until . . . slowly . . . but surely . . . she greatly reflected the famous statue.

Just so, the spiritual person seeks each day to conform to the image of Jesus Christ. A good question is, Am I more like Jesus Christ now than a year ago?

Perhaps you are a carnal person. You, too, can become a spiritual person by yielding your life to Jesus Christ, by acknowledging your self-centeredness and by making Jesus Christ supreme.

How? The Bible answers, "If we confess our sins, He is faithful and just to forgive us our sins and to cleanse us from all unrighteousness" (1 John 1:9).

QUESTIONS

1. Who is the natural man according to 1 Corinthians 2:14?
2. Why are the things of God meaningless to the natural man, according to 1 Corinthians 2:14?
3. List three characteristics of the carnal Christian according to 1 Corinthians 3:3.
4. Who is the spiritual man?
5. List two qualities of the spiritual man according to 1 Corinthians 2:15.

REMINDERS

God's divisions of mankind are based entirely upon the *spiritual condition* of the human heart!

"A sinning Christian is uncomfortable in the light of God's truth." —John MacArthur

The *natural man* is ego centered. He basically functions and seeks his fulfillment in the five human senses.

The natural man is one alienated from God, whereas the *carnal person* is a Christian under fleshly control.

The *spiritual man* is able to make right decisions, understand the Scriptures, and seeks to live according to God's will.

"These things I have written to you who believe in the name of the Son of God, that you may know that you have eternal life."

1 JOHN 5:13

"The Christian's relationship to God as a child to his Father is not only intimate, but sure. . . . So many people seem to do no more than hope for the best; is it possible to know for certain? It is. It is more than possible; it is God's revealed will for us. We ought to be sure of our relationship with God not just for the sake of our own peace of mind and helpfulness to others, but because God means us to be sure. John states categorically that this was his purpose in writing his first general Epistle. 'I write this to you who believe in the name of the Son of God, that you may know that you have eternal life'" (1 John 5:13)."[1]

JOHN R. W. STOTT, *BASIC CHRISTIANITY*

8

HOW TO BE SURE OF SALVATION

"CAN I REALLY BE SURE OF SALVA-TION?" That was a question asked by a young man overcome by doubt. He had lost all the peace he once knew and was now searching for some word of hope.

The Bible tells us that we can know—beyond a shadow of a doubt—that we are God's children. Assurance of salvation can be yours, right now—today.

It's shocking to realize how many people are made miserable by the disease called "doubt." Uncertainty has robbed thousands of people of the joy of salvation.

Even people who read their Bibles, earnestly pray, faithfully attend church, and live uprightly in their dealings with others may yet have no assurance of forgiveness and are living defeated lives.

Is assurance of salvation possible? What does the Bible say? In 2 Corinthians 13:5, Paul writes, "Examine yourselves as to whether you are in the faith." In

2 Peter 1:10 we are told, "Be even more diligent to make your calling and election sure." The assurance of salvation is one of God's beautiful gifts. Every believer ought to know that he possesses salvation.

Assurance is not only possible but necessary because it is that reality that brings purpose and power to our life. Christian assurance is a fortress of strength against the wiles of the devil. An uncertain salvation is a sad one that repels rather than attracts others. Assurance adds zeal and vitality to Christian service.

Assurance is not necessary for salvation, but it is necessary for an overcoming life. What does the word *assurance* actually mean? Assurance for the Christian is "The unwavering confidence of an intelligent faith in a present salvation." Having this knowledge is not only the privilege but the duty of every believer.

KNOWING BY THE WORD OF GOD

"How can I have this assurance?" you ask. We need to begin with the Bible. Assurance of salvation is based upon acceptance of the Bible as the unerring Word of God. As we apply the promises of the Bible to our lives, doubt leaves.

A Bible illustration of this truth is given to us in

the life of Abraham. Abraham received a promise from God that was humanly impossible, yet the Bible says, "He did not waver at the promise of God through unbelief" (Romans 4:20). We are also told that "Abraham believed God, and it was accounted to him for righteousness" (Galatians 3:6). The promises of God are as sure as God is.

The apostle John knew the difficulties of doubt. He saw many groping yet never finding, wishing but still waiting, looking yet still longing because of doubt. "These things I have written to you who believe in the name of the Son of God, *that you may know that you have eternal life*" (1 John 5:13). The object is that "you may know that you have eternal life." The word *know* means "to recognize the quality of." The apostle John wrote these verses so that we might recognize the quality of our position in Christ. This is not an opinion or a matter of inference but a revelation from God. Assurance is based on the truthfulness of God. Failure to believe is to make God a liar.

If you will sincerely trust God, fear will flee and your conscience will be calmed. Imagine a prisoner being offered a pardon. He reads the official document but is so overwhelmed that he is dazed by the news.

Suppose you ask, "Have you been pardoned?"
He would say, "Yes."
You might ask, "Do you feel pardoned?"
He replies, "No, I do not; it is so sudden."
"But," you ask, "if you do not feel pardoned, how can you know you are?"
"Oh," he says, as he points to the document, "this tells me so."

In the same way, the Bible is God's document of pardon to every believer.

COMMON MISCONCEPTIONS

Often there are misconceptions that make some Christians believe that assurance is impossible. A salesman friend said to me, "But I cannot know I am the Lord's till the day I die. It's presumptuous to be so certain."

I assured him that assurance is not arrogant presumption but a humble knowledge of a present acceptance by God. This confidence is based in the finished work of Christ. It is not self-confidence, for the Scripture says, "Not by works of righteousness which we have done, but according to His mercy He saved us" (Titus 3:5). My friend, is it presumptuous to accept what God has said?

The Philippian jailer called out, "What must I do to be saved?" (Acts 16:30). Paul answered, "Believe on the Lord Jesus Christ, and you will be saved" (v. 31). The Philippian jailer believed and was converted. Is it presumptuous to believe God?

You ask, "*What if I'm not one of the elect?*" Jesus said, "Whoever believes . . . should not perish but have eternal life" (John 3:16). That includes you! Salvation is offered to all. The Bible says that all men are sinners and that if we call upon the Lord, we shall be saved. Dwight L. Moody used to say, "The elect are the 'whosoever wills'; the non-elect are the 'whosoever won't's.'" Assurance is not the prerogative of a select few but all of God's people.

Others think they must know the day and the hour of their decision. This is wonderful to know but not necessary. A friend of mine was very concerned because she could not recall the exact time of her conversion. She was sure that she had received Christ as Savior and Lord but she didn't know when. I assured her that her assurance of salvation was more important than knowing the exact date she was converted.

"But," you say, "If you don't know the date, how can you be sure?'

May I ask, "How do you know you are alive physically?"

"Oh," you say, "I breathe, I eat, I think, I resolve."

So it is spiritually; if you have been converted, you will be interested in spiritual matters, you will breathe the atmosphere of heaven by praying, you will read the Bible, and you will be faithful in the local church where God has placed you. Should it be that your life is no different from the unconverted, then perhaps you have never been converted.

Then there are others who believe they must go through the valley of terror and tears before they can know. Tears that result in genuine repentance are beautiful, but mere tears of remorse are inadequate.

Our salvation rests upon facts. The Bible says, "For I delivered to you first of all that which I also received: that Christ died for our sins according to the Scriptures, and that He was buried, and that He rose again the third day according to the Scriptures" (1 Corinthians 15:3–4). These are the facts. After facts comes faith and then feelings. Many people lack assurance because they fail to realize a very important point: *faith brings assurance.*

KNOWING BY THE WITNESS WITHIN

Assurance of salvation is possible by the witness of the Holy Spirit. At your conversion, you became the dwelling place of the Holy Spirit. This heavenly guest wants complete lordship of your life. Yielding to the Holy Spirit brings definite assurance. Many, through carelessness and lack of knowledge, grieve the Holy Spirit and know little or nothing of the witness within. Paul the apostle said, "You received the Spirit of adoption by whom we cry out, 'Abba, Father.' The Spirit Himself bears witness with our spirit that we are children of God, and if children, then heirs— heirs of God and joint heirs with Christ" (Romans 8:15–17). What solid certainty this provides! Since God is our Father and we are His children, we cry, "Abba, Father," or literally, "My own dear Father." That cry is born of the Holy Spirit.

A. T. Pierson said, "When a child begins to talk, he uses the simplest consonants and the simplest vowels; and because he knows how to make but one syllable, he repeats the syllable. And so he says, 'papa' and 'mama.' The word for 'abba' is Aramaic for our word 'papa.'"[2]

Slavish fear is replaced with childlike love and the spirit of adoption rather than bondage. There is a father-child relationship, and we are in the family of God. Earthly parents are hurt by the mistrust of a child, and so doubt grieves the heart of God. Assurance rests primarily in the promises of God's Word, then subjectively in the experience of the believer. There is a danger here in making the experience of others the way for all.

The witness of the Spirit is the testimony of the indwelling Holy Spirit with our spirit that we are the children of God. The Holy Spirit opens our eyes to eternal values, enlightens our minds to perceive the truth, fills our hearts with divine love, gives compassion for others, makes intercession for us when we know not how to pray, comforts in the hours of tears, strengthens in the midst of battle, lifts us in the vale of defeat. These are some of the works of the Spirit in the believer. The Word of God says, "But the fruit of the Spirit is love, joy, peace, longsuffering, kindness, goodness, faithfulness, gentleness, self-control" (Galatians 5:22–23). If the fruit of the Spirit is in evidence, you may be sure of God's gracious work in your life.

A soldier lay dying on the battlefield. The chaplain asked, "What church are you of?"

"Of the church of Christ," he replied.

"I mean, what persuasion are you?"

"Persuasion!" said the wounded soldier as he looked upward. "I am persuaded that neither death nor life, nor angels nor principalities nor powers, nor things present nor things to come, nor height nor depth, nor any other created thing, shall be able to separate us from the love of God which is in Christ Jesus our Lord" (Romans 8:38–39).

At the conclusion of an evangelistic service, I was greeting people when a distinguished-looking man approached me and asked, "May I talk with you about my salvation? I'm desperately confused." He went on to state that he had acknowledged the Lord as Savior but had little peace and Christian confidence. "As I listened to your message, I decided I must settle it."

I replied, "First, look into your life to discover if all is right between yourself and the Lord. Carnal believers are usually full of doubts. If the Holy Spirit is grieved through self-will or sin, He cannot witness effectively to your salvation because there is contradiction. For this reason the witness of the Holy Spirit is often dimmed. Second, after discovering the wrong, openly confess it to the Lord. Third, deal with it and do work to prove your repentance."

"That's it!" he interrupted. "I've grown careless; there's sin in my life, and I must make it right."

We bowed our heads in a holy hush as he sought God's gracious forgiveness. It was evident that the Lord was in the room, for when we arose from our knees, the inquirer was changed. His expression, his voice, his whole attitude radiated blessed assurance. Careless living will always create doubt, but the opposite is also true. Doubt leads to careless living.

You will recall the story of Moses climbing Mount Sinai to receive the law. When he failed to return, the Israelites complained to Aaron, asking for Moses. Because Moses did not return, they doubted. On the heels of doubt followed sinful suggestions, and soon the Israelites danced around the golden calf. *Sinful living dims the witness of the Holy Spirit.*

KNOWING BY THE WORKS OF YOUR LIFE

Assurance of salvation is based upon the fruit of one's life. Let's look at some Bible tests.

1. *Obedience.* The first test is obedience. "Now by this we know that we know Him, if we keep His

commandments. He who says, 'I know Him,' and does not keep His commandments, is a liar, and the truth is not in him" (1 John 2:3–4).

Do you obey the Word of God? Jesus said, "If you love Me, keep My commandments" (John 14:15). "Why do you call Me, 'Lord, Lord,' and do not do the things which I say?" (Luke 6:46).

Is it your ambition to do the works of Christ? Do you delight in the law of the Lord? Are you a "doer of the Word"? Constant assurance depends upon practical obedience to the Word of God. Obedience is a good test, for Jesus said, "My sheep hear My voice, and I know them, and they follow Me" (John 10:27). Again, "Whoever fears Him and works righteousness is accepted by Him" (Acts 10:35).

2. *Love for the brethren.* Do you possess Christian love? A love for God's people is evidence of personal salvation. "He who says he is in the light, and hates his brother, is in darkness until now" (1 John 2:9). "For this is the message that you heard from the beginning, that we should love one another, not as Cain who was of the wicked one and murdered his brother" (1 John 3:11–12). Many professing Christians are destitute of love for others. The love test is important.

Perhaps at times you are not too sure you love the Lord. May I ask, "Do you love your mother?"

"Yes," you say.

"Well, how do you know?"

You say, "I show it by my affection and the things I do for her."

So also you may know whether you love the Lord by the things you do for Him. The natural man is at odds with God. "Everyone who loves is born of God and knows God" (1 John 4:7). Do you love fellow believers? "We know that we have passed from death to life, because we love the brethren" (1 John 3:14). "By this all will know that you are My disciples, if you have love for one another" (John 13:35).

3. *Love for God's Word.* Do you love God's Word? David said, "The statutes of the Lord are right, rejoicing the heart; the commandment of the Lord is pure, enlightening the eyes; the fear of the Lord is clean, enduring forever; the judgments of the Lord are true and righteous altogether. More to be desired are they than gold, yea, than much fine gold; sweeter also than honey and the honeycomb" (Psalm 19:8–10).

4. *Desire to worship.* Do you love God's house? "I

was glad when they said to me, 'Let us go into the house of the Lord'" (Psalm 122:1).

5. *Fruit of the Spirit.* Do you have the fruit of the Spirit? "But the fruit of the Spirit is love, joy, peace, longsuffering, kindness, goodness, faithfulness, gentleness, self-control. Against such there is no law" (Galatians 5:22–23).

After the apostle Paul met Christ, his life was proof of conversion. Love is difficult to hide. When a young man is in love, it is obvious. The same applies in the spiritual realm. As yourself again, "Do I love the Lord? Do I love His people? Do I love the Bible? Do I love to pray? Do I love God's house?" Your answer will help you to know where you stand.

All of us at times have passed through the sea of doubt. Bunyan speaks of being "much tumbled up and down in his thoughts." However, without question we may know now that we have eternal life. Jesus said, "He who believes in Me has everlasting life" (John 6:47). Anything that contradicts the words of Jesus is a lie. "Let God be true but every man a liar" (Romans 3:4).

Abraham, in the face of the unknown, had complete assurance. "By faith Abraham obeyed when he was called to go out to the place which he would receive as an inheritance. And he went out, not knowing where he was going. By faith he sojourned in the land of promise as in a foreign country, dwelling in tents with Isaac and Jacob, the heirs with him of the same promise; for he waited for the city which has foundations, whose builder and maker is God" (Hebrews 11:8–10).

David had full assurance: "I will see Your face in righteousness" (Psalm 17:15).

Daniel had glad assurance: "The people who know their God shall be strong" (Daniel 11:32).

Job had blessed assurance: "I know that my Redeemer lives" (Job 19:25).

Paul had abundant assurance: "I know whom I have believed and am persuaded that He is able to keep what I have committed to Him until that Day" (2 Timothy 1:12).

John the apostle believed in a "know-so" salvation: "These things I have written to you who believe in the name of the Son of God, that you may know that you have eternal life" (1 John 5:13). Millions have known this blessed assurance.

When that great Christian and scientist, Sir Michael Faraday, was dying, some journalists questioned him as to his speculations concerning the soul and death. "Speculations?" said the dying man in astonishment. "I know nothing about speculations; I'm resting on certainties. 'I know whom I have believed and am persuaded that He is able to keep what I have committed to Him until that Day'" (2 Timothy 1:12).

QUESTIONS

1. Is assurance of salvation possible? List two verses of Scripture to verify your answer.
2. What do we mean by the word *assurance*?
3. Can we possess assurance of salvation according to 1 John 5:13?
4. List four misconceptions regarding the assurance of salvation.
5. What do we mean by the witness of the Holy Spirit?
6. Is there a relationship of obedience to the witness of the Holy Spirit?
7. Assurance of salvation will be seen in at least four areas. What are they?

NOTES

1. John R. W. Stott, *Basic Christianity*, (Downers Grove, Ill: InterVarsity Press, 2008), 157–58.
2. A. T. Pierson, *The Heart of the Gospel* (New York: Baker & Taylor, 1892), 115.
3. P. B. Fitzwater, *Christian Theology* (Grand Rapids: Eerdmans, 1948), 458.

REMINDERS

Assurance for the Christian is "the unwavering confidence of an intelligent faith in a present salvation."

Assurance is based upon the truthfulness of God. Failure to believe is to make God a liar.

Yielding to the Holy Spirit brings definite assurance.

Sinful living dims the witness of the Holy Spirit.

Constant assurance depends upon practical obedience to the Word of God.

"To deny the possibility of assurance to the believer is to question, if not insult, the ability of the Holy Spirit."[3] —P. B. Fitzwater

"Do not love the world or the things in the world. If anyone loves the world, the love of the Father is not in him."

1 JOHN 2:15

"Anything that you love and do that keeps you from enjoying God's love and doing God's will is worldly and must be avoided."

WARREN WIERSBE, *WONDERFUL WORLD OF TEENS*

"The best contribution anyone can make to putting the world to rights is to live a Christian life, build a Christian home and radiate the light of the gospel of Jesus Christ."

JOHN R. W. STOTT, *BASIC CHRISTIANITY*

9

YOU AND
THE WORLD

A FAVORITE FEATURE IN *Reader's Digest,* almost since its beginning, has been the articles recalling "My Most Unforgettable Character." Sometimes well-known persons have been highlighted, but far more frequently these features have pointed to little-known men and women. They have been persons whose lives mattered in some special way because of their character, their personality, or of what they meant to others.

The true Christian is an unforgettable character who, day after day, is becoming more and more like the most unforgettable person the world has ever known. I speak, of course, of Jesus Christ.

The Christian life is not a matter of following a list of "dos" or observing a longer list of "don'ts." *The Christian life is a pledge of allegiance to Jesus Christ.* It is becoming so occupied with Him that the values of the world have little attraction.

If you have been born of God, if you have trusted Jesus Christ as your Savior, you have experienced a wonderful transformation. You are a new creature. You have a brand-new nature. You belong to a new family.

As a result, you have a new outlook. A new destination is now yours. Your whole attitude is changed.

During the Middle Ages, the Separatists believed that it was impossible to live a godly life unless they were isolated from the world about them. Their answer to worldliness was to build communities walled off from the society they tried to leave behind. As the years passed, however, the evils of civilization would move in on them, and a new start was again necessary.

Escape from the world is not possible. Nor should we want to escape. God wants us in the world for a holy purpose: to be witnesses for Jesus Christ. That is our ultimate reason for living in this world.

WHAT IS SEPARATION?

The Bible speaks of separation. For example, the apostle Paul instructed Christians at Corinth against involvement with the world around them. "Do not be unequally yoked together with unbelievers," he wrote in 2 Corinthians 6:14.

Like our society today, Corinth was evil. The very

name *Corinthian* became synonymous with lustful living. Even religious worship included immoral exhibitions.

With fatherly concern, the apostle wrote, "Come out from among them and be separate, says the Lord" (2 Corinthians 6:17). We are *in* the world but surely not *of* the world.

When the apostle tells us not to be yoked with unbelievers, he is referring to passages like Deuteronomy 22:9–11. Here we find the command, "You shall not sow your vineyard with different kinds of seed, lest the yield of the seed which you have sown and the fruit of your vineyard be defiled. You shall not plow with an ox and a donkey together. You shall not wear a garment of different sorts, such as wool and linen mixed together."

The principle here is simple: what God has joined, we should not separate; and what He has separated, we should not join.

Why does the Bible speak about unequal yoking? Because it is *unfitting* and *unfair.* The ox and the ass were different in size, temperament, and strength. The ox was also considered clean, whereas the ass was an unclean animal. Both would suffer discomfort and pain from unequal yoking. Harnessing them together formed a *poor working combination.*

> I appreciate the wisdom of John Koessler: "In the
> Scriptures the world is both the domain of Satan
> and the realm of the flesh. Whenever we behave
> in a 'worldly' fashion, we act in a way that is con-
> trary to Christ's interests. We are in the world, but
> we are not of it. Christ loves the world, but He
> does not love worldliness. The biblical notion of
> separation from the world is a positive concept. It
> is the result of a commitment to a personal rela-
> tionship with God through faith in Jesus Christ.
> In 1 John 1:5 the apostle warns that the love of
> worldliness and love for God are mutually exclu-
> sive. This means that the ultimate remedy for
> worldliness is a love for God."[1]

DEFINITE COMMANDS

But what is a Christian to do, and what is he not to
do? The Bible includes many definite commands.
Certain things are always right for the Christian. And
certain things are wrong. It is always right to be motivated by love for God and a needy world, but it is
always wrong to lie, to deceive, or to be governed by
evil motives.

Between the definite commands concerning good and evil, there is a definite no-man's land that at times presents a challenge. The Bible does not say "Thou shalt" or "Thou shalt not" concerning certain questions. In this realm, we need the Holy Spirit to apply the principles of the Bible to the particular subject.

At the moment of conversion, the Holy Spirit comes to dwell within you. His presence assures you of a living guide. He will help you evaluate your conduct according to God's will. However, always remember that our natures, at best, can be deceitful. In the face of doubt, it is necessary to call for help.

Often I have prayed, "Dear Lord, I am but a child. Help me to think right. Reveal Your will. Deliver me from evil and even the *appearance* of evil. Teach me to live in such a way that my conduct will glorify You." We need the Holy Spirit's help and we need to pray. But let me also suggest some guidelines.

BIBLE GUIDELINES

1. *Keep in mind the principle of ownership.* We who believe in Jesus have become God's children. We are twice His, in fact. He is our *Maker* and also our *Redeemer.* He has created us, and He has purchased us. Paul asks in 1 Corinthians 6:19, "Do you not know

that your body is the temple of the Holy Spirit who is in you, whom you have from God, and you are not your own?" He then goes on to explain: "You were bought at a price; therefore glorify God in your body" (v. 20). We do not belong to ourselves. God created us and redeemed us. Always remember the guideline of ownership.

2. *Our conduct should be governed by our awareness of responsibility for others.* We should ask ourselves, "How will my conduct affect those around me? Am I a stepping-stone or am I a stumbling block?" Never forget that the world knows that the Christian is different.

It was because of this principle that Paul wrote in 1 Corinthians 8:13, "Therefore, if food makes my brother stumble, I will never again eat meat, lest I make my brother stumble." The great apostle was determined to be a good and helpful example to others. The meat offered to the idols was probably the finest meat that money could buy. After it had been offered, it could be purchased cheaply in the open marketplace. But if eating this meat would offend others, Paul would refuse it. We must ask, "How will my lifestyle affect others?"

3. *Keep in mind the effect of your choices on your-*

self. This standard centers around your ability to count for God. We should ask, "Will my involvement make me more useful to God, or will it make me less useful? Can I ask His blessing upon this?"

Paul's application of this principle can be seen in 1 Corinthians 9:27, where he says, "I discipline my body and bring it into subjection, lest, when I have preached to others, I myself should become disqualified." Never forget the guideline of self. What will my involvement do to my personal effectiveness?

4. *Whatever we do should always be to the glory of God.* This is the all-important test. Always ask, "Can I do this for the glory of God?" Or, "What would Jesus Christ have me do?" The great apostle sums up this principle in 1 Corinthians 10:31: "Therefore, whether you eat or drink, or whatever you do, do all to the glory of God." The glory of God should be our supreme desire.

The Bible offers much help in discerning God's will in doubtful areas. First Thessalonians 5:22 sets forth a basic guideline: "Abstain from every form of evil."

Another is found in Romans 12:2: "And do not be conformed to this world, but be transformed by the renewing of your mind, that you may prove what is that good and acceptable and perfect will of God." We are to be *transformers* rather than *conformers.*

God's will is also mentioned in Galatians 1:4, which speaks of Christ "who gave Himself for our sins, that He might deliver us from this present evil age, according to the will of our God and Father."

Ephesians 6:12 describes our opposition: "For we do not wrestle against flesh and blood, but against principalities, against powers, against the rulers of the darkness of this age, against spiritual hosts of wickedness in the heavenly places."

James warns us in his epistle, "Do you not know that friendship with the world is enmity toward God?" Then he adds, "Whoever therefore wants to be a friend of the world makes himself an enemy of God" (James 4:4).

The apostle John in his gentle way gives a parallel warning in 1 John 2:15: "Do not love the world or the things in the world. If anyone loves the world, the love of the Father is not in him."

The person who is yielded to Jesus Christ will have overcome the problems of worldliness. Paul wrote in Galatians 2:20, "I have been crucified with Christ; it is no longer I who live, but Christ lives in me." In the final analysis, this moment-by-moment experience of letting Christ live in and through us is the answer to living a challenging Christian life.

"It is right for the church to be in the world; it is wrong for the world to be in the Church. A boat in water is good; that is what boats are for. However, water inside the boat causes it to sink."[2]

QUESTIONS

1. When Paul tells us in 2 Corinthians 6:14 not to be yoked with unbelievers, to which Old Testament passage is he referring?
2. Why does God forbid unequal yoking in Deuteronomy 22:10?
3. When the Bible does not clearly say, "Thou shalt," or "Thou shalt not," how are we to know what is of God?
4. List four guidelines for separation and the appropriate Scripture verses.
5. Why did Paul bring his body into subjection?
6. What is the all-important test?

NOTES

1. John Koessler, *True Discipleship* (Chicago: Moody, 2003), 280.
2. Harold Lindsell, *The World, the Flesh and the Devil* (Grand Rapids: Baker, 1975), 199.

REMINDERS

The Christian life is a pledge of allegiance to Jesus Christ. It is becoming so occupied with Him that the values and standards of the world around us have little influence.

Escape from the world is not possible. Nor should we want to escape. God wants us in the world for a holy purpose: to be witnesses for Jesus Christ.

"It is right for the church to be in the world; it is wrong for the world to be in the Church. A boat in water is good; that is what boats are for. However, water inside the boat causes it to sink." —Harold Lindsell

"In John 1:5 the apostle warns that the love of worldliness and love for God are mutually exclusive. This means that the ultimate remedy for worldliness is a love for God." —John Koessler

"Let us not give up meeting together, as some are in the habit of doing, but let us encourage one another—and all the more as you see the Day approaching."

HEBREWS 10:25 NIV

"The Bible knows nothing of solitary religion."

JOHN WESLEY

"Men may not read the gospel in seal-skin, or the gospel in morocco, or the gospel in cloth covers, but they can't get away from the gospel in shoe leather."

DONALD GREY BARNHOUSE

"Church attendance is as vital to a disciple as a transfusion of rich, healthy blood to a sick man."

DWIGHT L. MOODY

10

YOU AND
THE CHURCH

YOU NEED THE CHURCH AND the church
needs you. The Bible says we are living stones, joined
to one another in God's building. For real success in
the Christian life, every convert—and for that matter, every Christian—needs the fellowship of the
church, a divine permanent institution of which Jesus
said, "the gates of Hades shall not prevail against it"
(Matthew 16:18).

Someone has said, "Though the church has many
critics, it has not rivals." And despite the turmoil and
tribulation it may go through, despite the neglect it
may receive, the church will remain. It will survive
every onslaught and every attack because it belongs
to God (Matthew 16:18).

WHY IS THE CHURCH IMPORTANT?

The church is important because it is the organization of God, built upon the foundation of Jesus

Christ, and it will never pass away. It cannot be destroyed.

Jesus Christ is the foundation of the church. In Ephesians 1:22–23, we are told that God the Father has exalted Jesus Christ: "And [God] put all things under His feet, and gave Him to be head over all things to the church, which is His body, the fullness of Him who fills all in all."

The apostle Paul, in writing to the church at Corinth, emphasized the importance of this fact: "For no other foundation can anyone lay than that which is laid, which is Jesus Christ" (1 Corinthians 3:11). He instructed the believers at Ephesus that the proper love relationship between husband and wife should compare to the relationship of Christ to His church (see Ephesians 5:22–23).

One of the problems of the church is that it is made up of people like you and me. The church is a *divine institution* founded by Jesus, but it is also a *human institution*. It is not a hothouse operating under ideal conditions in a controlled atmosphere. It is an organized group of imperfect people, all of whom have faults and weaknesses.

We freely admit our faults and want to correct our weaknesses. But there is nothing God has given us, on earth or in heaven, that is more meaningful than the church.

WHAT IS THE CHURCH?

I am sure that when many people hear the word *church* they possibly think of a red-brick structure with a tall, impressive steeple. But the Bible never speaks of the church in this way.

Actually the Greek word *ekklesia*, which is translated "church" in the New Testament, refers to either a local gathering of Christian believers or else to the universal family of Christ made up of all people everywhere who have received Jesus as Savior. In 1 Corinthians 1:2 we read about "all who in every place call on the name of Jesus Christ our Lord." This refers to the *mystical body of Christ*, often called the *bride of Christ* or the church universal. However, this same verse begins, "To the church of God which is *at Corinth.*" This plainly refers to the local congregation of believers in the city of Corinth.

The word *ekklesia* is made up of two separate words—the preposition *ek*, meaning "out of," and the verb *kaleo*, meaning "to call." The church is *a called-out group of people*, a people separated by God unto Himself.

The English word *church* probably came from the Scottish word *kirk* or the German *kirche.* These, in turn, originated from the Greek word *kuriakon.* This word was used by the Greek Christians to designate a place of worship. It comes from the Greek word *Lord* and means that which is the Lord's place or the Lord's house.

When the word *ekklesia,* or *church,* is found in the New Testament, it generally refers to a body of believers banded together in a definite place; in other words, a particular group of people organized in a local community, accepting the Scriptures as the basis of faith and conduct.

P. T. Forsythe spoke of the local church as the "outcrop of the church universal." The local church is vital and is God's means of accomplishing His work here on earth.

A friend once told me, "I don't belong to a specific local church because I don't see that commanded in the Bible." But if that friend had studied his Bible seriously, he would have realized that the local assembly is strongly emphasized throughout the New Testament. The book of Acts implies that on the day of Pentecost 3,000 new believers were added to the church in Jerusalem. Later on in the book of

Acts, we read that the local church in Antioch commissioned Paul and Barnabas and sent them out as missionaries.

The apostle John received seven messages from the Lord Himself directed to seven *local* churches. Paul and his companions spent many years in the work of establishing and encouraging *local* assemblies. Nine of thirteen epistles he wrote under the direction of the Holy Spirit were addressed to *local* churches.

In our day it is the local church that sets apart missionaries and supports them. It is the local church that operates Sunday schools, helps the poor, and conducts services for worship, edification, and evangelism. It is the local church that serves as the human instrument to perform God's work here on earth. And it is because God's work must and will go on that there is a future for the church of Jesus Christ.

THE APOSTOLIC CHURCH

Chapter 2 of the book of Acts vividly relates the story of that first church in Jerusalem—how the Holy Spirit was poured out upon the 120 waiting believers. In Acts 2:41 we read, "Then those who gladly received his word were baptized; and that day about three thousand souls were added to them."

Those early believers *gladly received the Word of God.* They agreed with the Bible's indictment of guilt and sin, and they had an experience with the living Christ. And as a result of this salvation experience, they became a part of the 120 believers in Jerusalem: "Three thousand souls were added."

Christians down through the centuries have found that it is necessary to have fellowship together. The writer of Hebrews speaks of this when he refers to "not forsaking the assembling of ourselves together, as is the manner of some" (Hebrews 10:25). Martin Luther put it this way: "To gather with God's people in united adoration of the Father is as necessary to the Christian life as prayer."

Some time ago I suggested to a Christian man of many years that he ought to find a local church where he and his family could become active. "Oh," he said, "you don't have to be a member of a church to be a Christian."

Technically, he was right. Church membership has little to do with salvation. But in a practical aspect, he was wrong. I suggested to him that a man could also cross the ocean without the use of a plane or boat, but I wouldn't recommend it. I reminded him of the sharks he might encounter. The church is *God's vehicle* to carry us through the rough seas of our journey on earth. My friend, it is a colossal mistake to ignore the church!

You, my Christian friend, need the church and the church needs you!

WHY BE A CHURCH MEMBER?

From time to time I am confronted with excuses from people who will not become involved in the local church. "Church members have so many faults," some say. "There are so many hypocrites in the church." I am sure these things are true. There never was a perfect church—or a perfect Christian, for that matter. Even the first-century churches had their problems. People with problems need the church just like sick people need a hospital.

Once a person has received Jesus Christ as personal Savior, he needs to be *built up in the faith.* He needs to receive spiritual instruction and to share with other believers—to have opportunity for *Christian fellowship.* The church, through its ministries, is an instrument of training and provides an atmosphere for spiritual growth.

Every Christian needs the church and its people

in the dark hours of life. The fellowship of believers forms a vital unity in which there is strength and comfort. How many of God's people, overwhelmed with sorrow, have been undergirded by fellow Christians? Those who have passed through hard places can say and sing

> Blest be the tie that binds
> Our hearts in Christian love;
> The fellowship of kindred minds
> Is like to that above. —John Fawcett

Paul expressed his deep affection for the fellowship of other Christians. "I thank my God upon every remembrance of you . . . for your fellowship in the gospel from the first day until now" (Philippians 1:3–5). Yes, you need the church and the church needs you.

It is not enough to attend and contribute. You are needed—your godly example, your presence, your prayers, your influence, all that you are—these are needed. The ungodly do not hide their darkness, and we must not hide our light. The church urgently needs you.

WHAT IS THE MINISTRY
OF THE CHURCH?

The church is to assist its members to grow in every way possible. The church is a nursery to the newborn and a place of worship, education, and training for the mature believer.

It is interesting to observe the characteristics of the first church as presented in Acts 2:41–47. Within seventy years these Christians went over mountain peaks and tossing seas to rock the imperial city of Rome with the gospel of Jesus Christ. Acts 2 shows what this church possessed:

- A saved membership (v. 41)
- A steadfast membership (v. 42)
- A sacrificial membership (vv. 44–45)
- A serving membership (v. 46)
- A Spirit-filled membership (v. 47)

The postapostolic church was equally evangelistic. In the face of bitter persecution, the church marched forward to evangelize. Since we today enjoy apostolic succession, may we also experience apostolic success.

The Bible clearly teaches that *the program of the church is world evangelization.* Christ established the church in order to reach a lost world. The mission of the church is summed up in Christ's command: "Go therefore and make disciples of all the nations, baptizing them in the name of the Father and of the Son and of the Holy Spirit, teaching them to observe all things that I have commanded you; and lo, I am with you always, even to the end of the age" (Matthew 28:19–20).

Billions of people are included in this commission. The mission of the church is missions, and the mission of missions is the church. The last words of Jesus outlined the plan of action for the church: "You shall be witnesses to Me in Jerusalem, and in all Judea and Samaria, and to the end of the earth" (Acts 1:8). They were to begin at home. Peter and John witnessed the death and resurrection of Christ, and therefore they answered, "We cannot but speak the things which we have seen and heard" (Acts 4:20).

Today the need is greater than ever before. We, too, must share the gospel, for the charge of Christ is still our commission today. Let us proclaim the gospel in season and out of season, in the highways and the hedges, in public and private, from January to December, every day of the week, every week of every month, every month of every year, till the job is done. The unbreakable promise of Christ is, "And lo, I am with you always, even to the end of the age" (Matthew 28:20).

QUESTIONS

1. Why is the church important, according to Matthew 16:18 and Ephesians 1:22?
2. What is the church?
3. Explain the difference between the local church and the church universal, according to 1 Corinthians 1:2.
4. List a few reasons why believers should be members of a local group.
5. List five characteristics of the apostolic church as given in Acts 2:41–47.
6. Though the church exists to help believers grow, what is the program of the church concerning the world?

REMINDERS

D. L. Moody said, "Church attendance is as vital to a disciple as a transfusion of rich, healthy blood to a sick man."

According to the Word of God, the church is a permanent, divine institution that shall never be destroyed (Matthew 16:18).

One of the problems of the church is that it is made up of people like you and me. The church is a *divine institution*, founded by Jesus, but it is also a *human institution*. It is not a hothouse operating under ideal conditions in a controlled atmosphere. It is an organized group of imperfect saints, all of whom have faults and weaknesses.

The church is a *called-out group of people*, a people separated by God unto Himself.

There never was a perfect church—or a perfect Christian, for that matter.

People with problems need the church just like sick people need a hospital.

11

YOU AND
YOUR MONEY

I WILL ALWAYS REMEMBER MY Scottish mother, with her strong brogue, urging her children to "seldom repress a generous impulse!" She taught us to be generous in life and only seldom . . . seldom . . . repress being generous!

When we asked why we should be generous, she answered because "our God is a generous God" (James 1:5, 17).

Giving for the Christian is a joyful privilege rather than an obligation.

Giving cannot be separated from the gospel. The gospel, in fact, is giving. It is in the center of John 3:16: "For God so loved the world that He gave His only begotten Son."

God gave, and we too want to give. That is the core of what the apostle Paul is saying in 2 Corinthians. To challenge and possibly to shame the Corinthian believers, he tells how believers in Macedonia, in spite of "a great trial of affliction" and "deep poverty" (2 Corinthians 8:2), begged for a share in helping needy Christians at Jerusalem.

Years before, on the Asiatic side of the Aegean Sea, Paul had experienced his Macedonian vision. The call had been, "Come over to Macedonia and help us" (Acts 16:9).

Now there had been a second call. Not, "Come over and help us," but "Come over and take our help to others."

For the Macedonian Christians, giving was not a chore but a challenge, not a burden but a blessing. Giving was not something to be avoided but a privilege to be desired. The danger for these Macedonians was not that they would give too little but that they would give too much.

Suffering at times produces selfishness, for too often we take special care of ourselves and forget others. Not so with these Christians. They experienced great trials and deep poverty, but this double yoke could not cramp their large heartedness.

The way they gave is also notable: "not only as we had hoped, but they first gave themselves to the Lord, and then to us by the will of God" 2 Corinthians 8:5.

Notice the sequence. The first step in Christian

giving is not our money but *ourselves*! Then sharing *what we have* will follow.

THE TITHE

But some may ask, "What about the tithe?" The tithe, according to the Bible, is one-tenth of a person's possessions. People often dismiss tithing with the casual remark, "We are not under law but grace."

That statement is true, but, remember, the gospel of grace goes beyond the law. The law declares, "Thou shalt not kill" (Exodus 20:13 KJV), but the gospel says, "Thou shalt not hate," and even more, "Thou shalt love."

The law of Moses demanded one-seventh of the individual's time and one-tenth of his income for God. That was the minimum. The tithe is the starting place, not the goal. Likewise today, the tithe is a starting place, not the goal. The gospel of grace goes beyond the tithe.

Every new convert will want to do under grace at least what was required under law. Herschel Hobbs has said, "The nine-tenths prove man's love, but the one-tenth tests man's legal obedience."[1] Make your money immortal: "Lay up for yourselves treasures in heaven" (Matthew 6:20).

Giving should be *systematic*. First Corinthians

16:2 says, "On the first day of the week let each one of you lay something aside, storing up as he may prosper." At the very beginning of your Christian life, acquire the habit of regular giving.

In addition to giving systematically, we should give cheerfully. To have a part in God's program is a happy privilege. Paul puts it this way: "So let each one give as he purposes in his heart, not grudgingly or of necessity; for God loves a cheerful giver" (2 Corinthians 9:7).

When we come to the end of life, the question will be, "How much have you given?" not, "How much have you gotten?" It will be "How much have you sacrificed?" not, "How much have you saved?" We are to be givers rather than getters.

CHRIST'S EXAMPLE

According to 2 Corinthians 8:1, all giving *begins* with "the grace of God." God's generosity to the churches of Macedonia enabled and motivated their generosity.

GIVING BEGINS WITH GOD!

The motive for all Christian giving is summed up beautifully in 2 Corinthians 8:9: "For you know the grace of our Lord Jesus Christ, that though He was rich, yet for your sakes He became poor, that you through His poverty might become rich."

Four truths are plain. He was rich; we were poor. He became poor; we became rich. Let's think about these great facts for a moment.

1. *He was rich.* In the beginning, when all was dark, God spoke and spun all creation into being. God said, "Let there be light" (Genesis 1:3), and the sun was set afire in the skies.

He spangled the night with the beaming moon and shimmering stars. Then, between day and night, He placed the world and started it on its journey around the sun.

Then God scooped out the valleys and bulged up the mountains. God cooled the hot earth with water, dividing the land from the seas. Then the flowers blossomed. Fruit trees produced. Herbs sprouted.

After this, God placed living creatures on the earth—beasts of every kind. "And God saw that it was good" (Genesis 1:25).

Finally, God made man. He breathed into him His breath, and man became a living soul. All creation declares the Creator's might and wisdom.

God is rich in power. All the silver and gold belongs to Him. The diamonds in the black caverns of earth are His. The cattle on a thousand hills belong to Him.

He is rich in wisdom. He is omniscient. The past, present, and future are one eternal *now* to Him. He is rich in life. When He came to earth and took the form of man, death had no claim on Him. He is God from everlasting to everlasting.

2. *We are poor.* How poor are we? So poor that we have nothing with which to plead in heaven's courts. We are so poor that we could not afford a lawyer to plead our case, so poor that we have no robes to cover our guilt. Romans 3 spells out the sorry story:

> As it is written: "There is none righteous, no, not one . . . none who seeks after God. They have all turned aside; they have together become unprofitable; there is none who does good, no, not one. Their throat is an open tomb; with their tongues they have practiced deceit; the poison of asps is under their lips; whose mouth is full of cursing and bitterness. Their feet are swift to shed blood; destruction and misery are in their ways; and the way of peace they have not known." (vv. 10–17)

We were poor. How poor? So poor that we had no medicine that would cleanse our sin. So poor that we could find no bread or water for our thirsty soul.

3. *He became poor.* Jesus Christ is the supreme example of giving: "Though He was rich, yet for your sakes He became poor, that you through His poverty might become rich" (2 Corinthians 8:9).

How poor did He become? He was so poor that there was no place for Him to be born. He was born in a stable with the cattle as His witnesses.

Think how He could have come. He could have been born in a palace, rocked in a golden cradle, fed with a golden spoon. He could have had angels as His attendants.

But no. As Philippians 2 tells us, He "made Himself of no reputation, taking the form of a bondservant, and coming in the likeness of men. And being found in appearance as a man, He humbled Himself and became obedient to the point of death, even the death of the cross" (vv. 7–8).

How poor was He? So poor that, even though He had made the world, He had no place to dwell. The ground was His couch, the rocks His pillow, the brook His washbasin, the breeze His towel, and the wind His comb.

One day He spoke to a multitude, and we read that after He had finished "everyone went to his own house" (John 7:53). But the same gospel narrative goes on to say that "Jesus went to the Mount of Olives" (8:1).

When He died, it was as a poor man, crucified between two criminals. He was so poor that He had to commit His mother to another's care. When it was time for the burial, He was not buried in His own tomb but the tomb of another.

Why did He become poor? "For your sakes"—for the sake of those who were lost—for those who were poor. For me. For you.

4. *We become rich.* How rich do we become? As rich as Jesus Christ Himself. We were dead—without hope—but we are now alive, children of God. We are not only children but heirs. We are priests and kings, and we shall reign with Him.

How rich do we become? All the wealth that is His becomes ours. We are joint heirs with God. Triumphantly we can sing:

My Father is rich in houses and lands,
He holdeth the wealth of the world in His hands!
Of rubies and diamonds, of silver and gold,

His coffers are full, He has riches untold.
—*Harriet E. Buell*

Yes, and these riches are ours, and we can say,

I'm a child of the King,
A child of the King,
With Jesus my Saviour,
I'm a child of the King.
—*Harriet E. Buell*

He has made us rich, so what shall we give in return? What shall I do with this life of mine—my money, my time? Shall I withhold it? Dare I withhold it? What will you do?

Remember, the grace of our Lord Jesus Christ!

Because we forget so quickly, Paul urges the Macedonian Christians, *to finish* and *complete* what they had begun. "But now *finish* doing it also, so that just as there was a readiness to desire it, so there may be also *the completion of it* by your ability" 2 Corinthians 8:11 NASB).

QUESTIONS

1. Did Jesus speak often of giving?
2. According to 2 Corinthians 8:5, how did the Macedonian Christians give?
3. List two things that should characterize our giving according to 1 Corinthians 16:2.
4. According to 2 Corinthians 8:9, who is the supreme example of giving?
5. How did Jesus Christ assume our poverty?
6. Share something about our riches as the children of God.

NOTES

1. Herschel Hobbs, *The Gospel of Giving* (Nashville: Broadman, 1954), 13).

REMINDERS

Seldom repress a generous impulse!

All giving begins with "the grace of God" (2 Corinthians 8:1).

According to Leslie B. Flynn, "Money not only talks; 'it screams.'"

In seventeen of His thirty-seven parables, Jesus dealt with property and man's responsibility for using it wisely.

For the Macedonian Christians, giving was not a chore but a challenge, not a burden but a blessing. Giving was not something to be avoided but a privilege to be desired.

The Dead Sea is a dead sea because it continually receives and *never gives*.

When we come to the end of life, the question will be, "How much have you given?" not, "How much have you gotten?"

Jesus Christ is the supreme example of giving.

The apostle Paul urged the Macedonian Christians to keep their promise and "finish" what they had begun (2 Corinthians 8:11 NASB).

12

SCRIPTURE PROMISES FOR SPIRITUAL PROBLEMS

WHEN YOU RECEIVED JESUS CHRIST as your Savior, you became a member of the family of God. As a child of God, your wealth increased, for you inherited thousands of guaranteed promises. May I encourage you to *read them, believe them, and live in the reality of them.*

HELPFUL SUGGESTIONS

1. Read these promises from God's Word and memorize as many as possible. I often type them out on note cards and carry them with me so that I can memorize God's Word whenever I have some unexpected free time.

2. Accept these promises as they are. For the most part, do not spiritualize. Someone has said,

"Those who spiritualize tell spiritual lies, because they lack spiritual eyes."

3. Do your part. If the promise says "repent," then repent. If it says "pray," then pray.

4. Commit your life and area of need to the Lord. He is totally trustworthy. The promise may be fulfilled immediately or the answer may be delayed, but the important thing is that we lay our cares at His feet. With Paul we can enthusiastically say that we are "fully convinced that what He had promised He was also able to perform" (Romans 4:21).

ANSWERS TO PRAYER

"Call upon Me in the day of trouble; I will deliver you, and you shall glorify Me" (Psalm 50:15).

"Evening and morning and at noon I will pray, and cry aloud, and He shall hear my voice" (Psalm 55:17).

"Therefore I say to you, whatever things you ask when you pray, believe that you receive them, and you will have them" (Mark 11:24).

"For everyone who asks receives, and he who seeks finds, and to him who knocks it will be opened" (Luke 11:10).

"If you abide in Me, and My words abide in you, you will ask what you desire, and it shall be done for you" (John 15:7).

THE BIBLE

"Forever, O Lord, Your word is settled in heaven" (Psalm 119:89).

"The grass withers, the flower fades, but the word of our God stands forever" (Isaiah 40:8).

"All Scripture is given by inspiration of God, and is profitable for doctrine, for reproof, for correction, for instruction in righteousness" (2 Timothy 3:16).

"Your word is a lamp to my feet and a light to my path" (Psalm 119:105).

"Be diligent to present yourself approved to God, a worker who does not need to be ashamed, rightly dividing the word of truth" (2 Timothy 2:15).

"So then faith comes by hearing, and hearing by the word of God" (Romans 10:17).

CHRIST'S RETURN

"Looking for the blessed hope and glorious appearing of our great God and Savior Jesus Christ" (Titus 2:13).

"Beloved, now we are children of God; and it has not yet been revealed what we shall be, but we know that when He is revealed, we shall be like Him, for we shall see Him as He is" (1 John 3:2).

"Therefore judge nothing before the time, until the Lord comes, who will both bring to light the hidden things of darkness and reveal the counsels of the hearts. Then each one's praise will come from God" (1 Corinthians 4:5).

"For the Lord Himself will descend from heaven with a shout, with the voice of an archangel, and with the trumpet of God. And the dead in Christ will rise first. Then we who are alive and remain shall be caught up together with them in the clouds to meet the Lord in the air. And thus we shall always be with the Lord" (1 Thessalonians 4:16–17).

CLEANSING

"If we confess our sins, He is faithful and just to forgive us our sins and to cleanse us from all unrighteousness" (1 John 1:9).

"But if we walk in the light as He is in the light, we have fellowship with one another, and the blood of Jesus Christ His Son cleanses us from all sin" (1 John 1:7).

"But He was wounded for our transgressions, He was bruised for our iniquities; the chastisement for our peace was upon Him, and by His stripes we are healed" (Isaiah 53:5).

"And according to the law almost all things are purified with blood, and without shedding of blood there is no remission" (Hebrews 9:22).

"In Him we have redemption through His blood, the forgiveness of sins, according to the riches of His grace" (Ephesians 1:7).

ETERNAL LIFE

"For God so loved the world that He gave His only begotten Son, that whoever believes in Him should not perish but have everlasting life" (John 3:16).

"Most assuredly, I say to you, he who hears My word and believes in Him who sent Me has everlasting life, and shall not come into judgment, but has passed from death to life" (John 5:24).

"My sheep hear My voice, and I know them, and they follow Me. And I give them eternal life, and they shall never perish; neither shall anyone snatch them out of My hand" (John 10:27–28).

"These things I have written to you who believe in the name of the Son of God, that you may know that you have eternal life" (1 John 5:13).

FAMILY

"Train up a child in the way he should go, and when he is old he will not depart from it" (Proverbs 22:6).

"Then I will give them one heart and one way, that they may fear Me forever, for the good of them and their children after them" (Jeremiah 32:39).

"'Honor your father and mother,' which is the first commandment with promise: 'that it may be well with you and you may live long on the earth'" (Ephesians 6:2–3).

"Children, obey your parents in all things, for this is well pleasing to the Lord" (Colossians 3:20).

FEAR

"Fear not, for I am with you; be not dismayed, for I am your God. I will strengthen you, yes, I will help you, I will uphold you with My righteous right hand" (Isaiah 41:10).

"Then the angel said to them, 'Do not be afraid, for behold, I bring you good tidings of great joy which will be to all people'" (Luke 2:10).

"But immediately Jesus spoke to them, saying, 'Be of good cheer! It is I; do not be afraid'" (Matthew 14:27).

"Brethren, I do not count myself to have apprehended; but one thing I do, forgetting those things which are behind and reaching forward to those things which are ahead" (Philippians 3:13).

"Not that we are sufficient of ourselves to think of anything as being from ourselves, but our sufficiency is from God" (2 Corinthians 3:5).

FINANCES

"And my God shall supply all your need according to His riches in glory by Christ Jesus" (Philippians 4:19).

"Now if God so clothes the grass of the field, which today is, and tomorrow is thrown into the oven, will He not much more clothe you, O you of little faith?" (Matthew 6:30).

FRUSTRATION

"Commit your way to the Lord, trust also in Him, and He shall bring it to pass" (Psalm 37:5).

"Let us therefore come boldly to the throne of grace, that we may obtain mercy and find grace to help in time of need" (Hebrews 4:16).

HEAVEN

"Jesus answered and said to him, 'If anyone loves Me, he will keep My word; and My Father will love him, and We will come to him and make Our home with him'" (John 14:23).

"Then we who are alive and remain shall be caught up together with them in the clouds to meet the Lord in the air. And thus we shall always be with the Lord" (1 Thessalonians 4:17).

"There shall be no night there: They need no lamp nor light of the sun, for the Lord God gives them light. And they shall reign forever and ever" (Revelation 22:5).

HOLINESS

"If anyone defiles the temple of God, God will destroy him. For the temple of God is holy, which temple you are" (1 Corinthians 3:17).

"Therefore 'come out from among them and be separate, says the Lord. Do not touch what is unclean, and I will receive you. I will be a Father to you, and you shall be My sons and daughters, says the Lord Almighty'" (2 Corinthians 6:17–18).

"Therefore, having these promises, beloved, let us cleanse ourselves from all filthiness of the flesh and spirit, perfecting holiness in the fear of God" (2 Corinthians 7:1).

HOPE

"For You are my hope, O Lord God; You are my trust from my youth" (Psalm 71:5).

"And the Lord shall help them and deliver them; He shall deliver them from the wicked, and save them, because they trust in Him" (Psalm 37:40).

"Through whom also we have access by faith into this grace in which we stand, and rejoice in hope of the glory of God" (Romans 5:2).

"Now hope does not disappoint, because the love of God has been poured out in our hearts by the Holy Spirit who was given to us" (Romans 5:5).

HOSPITALIZATION

"Likewise the Spirit also helps in our weaknesses. For we do not know what we should pray for as we ought, but the Spirit Himself makes intercession for us with groanings which cannot be uttered" (Romans 8:26).

"Beloved, I pray that you may prosper in all things and be in health, just as your soul prospers" (3 John 2).

"He delivers the poor in their affliction, and opens their ears in oppression" (Job 36:15).

"Behold, I am the Lord, the God of all flesh. Is there anything too hard for Me?" (Jeremiah 32:27).

LONELINESS

"Let your conduct be without covetousness, and be content with such things as you have. For He Himself has said, 'I will never leave you nor forsake you'" (Hebrews 13:5).

"For the Lord will not cast off His people, nor will He forsake His inheritance" (Psalm 94:14).

"When my father and my mother forsake me, then the Lord will take care of me" (Psalm 27:10).

"And He said, 'My Presence will go with you, and I will give you rest'" (Exodus 33:14).

NERVOUSNESS

"Peace I leave with you, My peace I give to you; not as the world gives do I give to you. Let not your heart be troubled, neither let it be afraid" (John 14:27).

"Have I not commanded you? Be strong and of good courage; do not be afraid, nor be dismayed, for the Lord your God is with you wherever you go" (Joshua 1:9).

"Whenever I am afraid, I will trust in You" (Psalm 56:3).

PEACE

"Blessed are the peacemakers, for they shall be called sons of God" (Matthew 5:9).

"Finally, brethren, farewell. Become complete. Be of good comfort, be of one mind, live in peace; and the God of love and peace will be with you" (2 Corinthians 13:11).

"Behold, how good and how pleasant it is for brethren to dwell together in unity!" (Psalm 133:1).

"And the peace of God, which surpasses all understanding, will guard your hearts and minds through Christ Jesus" (Philippians 4:7).

PERSECUTION

"Blessed are those who are persecuted for righteousness' sake, for theirs is the kingdom of heaven" (Matthew 5:10).

"If we endure, we shall also reign with Him. If we deny Him, He also will deny us" (2 Timothy 2:12).

"For our light affliction, which is but for a moment, is working for us a far more exceeding and eternal weight of glory" (2 Corinthians 4:17).

"We are hard-pressed on every side, yet not crushed; we are perplexed, but not in despair; persecuted, but not forsaken; struck down, but not destroyed" (2 Corinthians 4:8–9).

PRESENCE OF THE LORD

"For the Lord God is a sun and shield; the Lord will give grace and glory; no good thing will He withhold from those who walk uprightly" (Psalm 84:11).

"Teaching them to observe all things that I have commanded you; and lo, I am with you always, even to the end of the age" (Matthew 28:20).

"And He said, 'My Presence will go with you, and I will give you rest'" (Exodus 33:14).

PRESERVATION

"Now to Him who is able to keep you from stumbling, and to present you faultless before the presence of His glory with exceeding joy" (Jude 24).

"Who are kept by the power of God through faith for salvation ready to be revealed in the last time" (1 Peter 1:5).

"For I am persuaded that neither death nor life, nor angels nor principalities nor powers, nor things present nor things to come, nor height nor depth, nor any other created thing, shall be able to separate us from the love of God which is in Christ Jesus our Lord" (Romans 8:38–39).

PROTECTION

"The Lord is my light and my salvation; whom shall I fear? The Lord is the strength of my life; of whom shall I be afraid?" (Psalm 27:1).

"Of Benjamin he said: 'The beloved of the Lord shall dwell in safety by Him, who shelters him all the day long; and he shall dwell between His shoulders'" (Deuteronomy 33:12).

"God is our refuge and strength, a very present help in trouble" (Psalm 46:1).

"For this reason I also suffer these things; nevertheless I am not ashamed, for I know whom I have believed and am persuaded that He is able to keep what I have committed unto Him against that Day" (2 Timothy 1:12).

RESURRECTION

"In a moment, in the twinkling of an eye, at the last trumpet. For the trumpet will sound, and the dead will be raised incorruptible, and we shall be changed" (1 Corinthians 15:52).

"Jesus said to her, 'I am the resurrection and the life. He who believes in Me, though he may die, he shall live'" (John 11:25).

SICKNESS

"And His disciples asked Him, saying, 'Rabbi, who sinned, this man or his parents, that he was born blind?' Jesus answered, 'Neither this man nor his parents sinned, but that the works of God should be revealed in him'" (John 9:2–3).

"Likewise the Spirit also helps in our weaknesses. For we do not know what we should pray for as we ought, but the Spirit Himself makes intercession for us with groanings which cannot be uttered. Now He who searches the hearts knows what the mind of the Spirit is, because He makes intercession for the saints according to the will of God" (Romans 8:26–27).

"Concerning this thing I pleaded with the Lord three times that it might depart from me. And He said to me, 'My grace is sufficient for you, for My strength is made perfect in weakness.' Therefore most gladly I will rather boast in my infirmities, that the power of Christ may rest upon me" (2 Corinthians 12:8–9).

"Is anyone among you suffering? Let him pray. Is anyone cheerful? Let him sing psalms. Is anyone among you sick? Let him call for the elders of the church, and let them pray over him, anointing him with oil in the name of the Lord. And the prayer of faith will save the sick, and the Lord will raise him up. And if he has committed sins, he will be forgiven" (James 5:13–15).

SLEEPLESSNESS

"The Lord will command His lovingkindness in the daytime, and in the night His song shall be with me— a prayer to the God of my life" (Psalm 42:8).

"I lay down and slept; I awoke, for the Lord sustained me" (Psalm 3:5).

"I will both lie down in peace, and sleep; for You alone, O Lord, make me dwell in safety" (Psalm 4:8).

SORROW

"If He takes away, who can hinder Him? Who can say to Him, 'What are You doing?'" (Job 9:12).

"Those who trust in the Lord are like Mount Zion, which cannot be moved, but abides forever" (Psalm 125:1).

"But He knows the way that I take; when He has tested me, I shall come forth as gold" (Job 23:10).

STRENGTH

"But you shall receive power when the Holy Spirit has come upon you; and you shall be witnesses to Me in Jerusalem, and in all Judea and Samaria, and to the end of the earth" (Acts 1:8).

"Trust in the Lord forever, for in YAH, the Lord, is everlasting strength" (Isaiah 26:4).

"But those who wait on the Lord shall renew their strength; they shall mount up with wings like eagles, they shall run and not be weary, they shall walk and not faint" (Isaiah 40:31).

"So he answered and said to me: 'This is the word of the Lord to Zerubbabel:" Not by might nor by power, but by My Spirit,' says the Lord of hosts"'" (Zechariah 4:6).

TEMPTATION

"No temptation has overtaken you except such as is common to man; but God is faithful, who will not allow you to be tempted beyond what you are able, but with the temptation will also make the way of escape, that you may be able to bear it" (1 Corinthians 10:13).

"These things I have spoken to you, that in Me you may have peace. In the world you will have tribulation; but be of good cheer, I have overcome the world" (John 16:33).

"Therefore submit to God. Resist the devil and he will flee from you" (James 4:7).

WISDOM

"If any of you lacks wisdom, let him ask of God who gives to all liberally and without reproach, and it will be given to him" (James 1:5).

"Many people shall come and say, 'Come and let us go up to the mountain of the Lord, to the house of the God of Jacob; He will teach us His ways, and we shall walk in His paths.' For out of Zion shall go forth the law, and the word of the Lord from Jerusalem" (Isaiah 2:3).

"The fear of the Lord is the beginning of wisdom, and the knowledge of the Holy One is understanding" (Proverbs 9:10).

HOW TO FINISH
THE CHRISTIAN LIFE

978-0-8024-3588-0

Dr. George Sweeting's *How to Begin the Christian Life* revealed a plan for success in starting new lives of purpose in pursuit of Christ. Now he and his son, Donald Sweeting, present *How to Finish the Christian Life*, a guide that gives mature believers a new set of disciplines and encouraging truths to help them finish well. Dr. Sweeting and his son deliver the inspiring message that the second half of the believer's journey should be seen as a challenge to live to the fullest for the glory of God.

Also available as an eBook

MOODY
PUBLISHERS

How to Continue
the Christian Life

Avaliable March 2013

978-0-8024-3601-6

In this concise resource, respected evangelist and teacher George Sweeting instructs believers how to press on in following Jesus through all of life. Starting where his best-selling book *How to Begin the Christian Life* leaves off, Dr. Sweeting walks the believer through the Christian life from the first days of faith to a life of faithful discipleship. He emphasizes the work of the Holy Spirit in saving and growing the believer as well as the role of the believer to faithfully pursue Jesus through prayer and interaction with God's Word.

Also available as an eBook

MOODY
PUBLISHERS

www.MoodyPublishers.com